W. Ellis Hume-Williams

The Irish Parliament from the Year 1782 to 1800

Being the Cressingham Prize Essay, 1878

W. Ellis Hume-Williams

The Irish Parliament from the Year 1782 to 1800
Being the Cressingham Prize Essay, 1878

ISBN/EAN: 9783337154806

Printed in Europe, USA, Canada, Australia, Japan

Cover: Foto ©Suzi / pixelio.de

More available books at **www.hansebooks.com**

THE IRISH PARLIAMENT

FROM

THE YEAR 1782 TO 1800.

BEING THE

CRESSINGHAM PRIZE ESSAY
1878.

BY

W. ELLIS HUME WILLIAMS, ESQ.

UNDERGRADUATE, TRINITY HALL.

"NOTHING EXTENUATE
NOR SET DOWN AUGHT IN MALICE."

CASSELL PETTER & GALPIN,
LONDON, PARIS & NEW YORK.
1879.

LONDON:
PRINTED BY THE ARTISTIC COLOUR-PRINTING COMPANY LIMITED,
PLAYHOUSE YARD, BARBICAN, E.C.

TO

THE RIGHT HONOURABLE

Hugh MacCalmont, Earl Cairns,

LORD HIGH CHANCELLOR OF GREAT BRITAIN.

THIS ESSAY

IS

RESPECTFULLY DEDICATED.

PREFACE.

The Author has thought it desirable to preface this essay on the Irish Parliament from the years 1782 to 1800, by a brief review of its antecedent condition, and by special quotation of the correspondence between the Irish Viceroy and the English Premier at the close of 1782.

It is difficult to estimate the utterances and action of the Irish or English Parliaments during that period, apart from the Social and Political influences coincident with them. These the Author has endeavoured to treat of with as much brevity as their importance permitted.

The present cry of Home Rule and agitation for Irish Volunteer organisation, lend fresh interest to past Irish history. The advocates of both may find their best response in its study.

Trinity Hall,
   Cambridge,
      May, 1879.

"Irish Policy is Irish History, and I have no faith in any Statesman who attempts to remedy the evils of Ireland who is either ignorant of the past or will not take lessons from it."—*Disraeli, 1868.*

IN attempting an impartial consideration of the most eventful period of Irish history, it is essential to commence by examining the social and political condition of the country at the time. By tracing events both at home and abroad, we shall be enabled to form a just estimate of that combination of circumstances which was the precursor, if not the direct cause, of the crisis resulting in Irish Parliamentary Independence.

To begin with England. In the Spring of 1782, the Ministry of Lord North was brought to an abrupt termination. The position of the country at the close of his twelve years' administration was without precedent. Impolicy and injustice had borne full fruits in blunders and disasters. Political disappointments and military reverses afforded to a powerful Opposition ample justification for continual assaults. Ministerial majorities decreased in number and in quality. Fox and Burke, unceasing in their attacks, not only on the measures of the Government, but also on the capacity and personal character of its leader, at length forced his resignation. Much of the calamity which attended Lord North's administration must be attributed to the conflict between principles and measures, marking the efforts of the Premier to reconcile the caprices and prejudices of his Sovereign with the interests and requirements of the State. Friends were thereby alienated, foes were not conciliated. The favour of the King proved powerless against the dissatisfaction of the people. The Royal threats of abdication in March, 1778,

B

"rather than submit to be trampled on by his enemies," which in reality meant "rather than loosen his failing grasp on America," repeated four years after when a Whig coalition was proposed, were far from bearing their expected fruits. Popular feeling and personal loyalty had been strained to their uttermost. It was felt that the prerogative of the Crown had overridden the responsibility of the Minister. The writings of Junius were still fresh in the public mind; he had taught them that "the ruin or prosperity of a State depends so much upon the administration of its Government, that, to be acquainted with the merits of a Ministry, we need only observe the condition of the people." By this standard was Lord North judged. In our American colonies open discontent had ripened into revolt, the disasters of which culminated in the submission of Cornwallis, and ended in the declaration of Independence. Our Empire in the East was threatened with destruction, as the arms of Coote had not yet prevailed. Hyder Ali, twice defeated, was still a formidable foe. The triumphs of Warren Hastings were also incomplete. Britain stood alone against the united powers of France, Spain and Holland. France was eager for revenge for her expulsion from Canada and India; Spain was snatching at Gibraltar, where destruction was awaiting her fleet; while Holland was content to make her islands the storehouse for our foes. Our West Indian Islands were ravaged, and our trade in these seas swept away by the enemy's marine, for the gallant Howe or Rodney had not yet given our foes their lesson and re-assumed for England the sovereignty of the sea. The few ships that could be spared for the purpose were not sufficient to prevent English coasts and harbours from being insulted, as privateers hovered about the Channel and made easy prey of passing merchandise. On the Continent dissatisfaction was fast ripening into absolute revolution; the air was heavy with rumours, and the hearts of many failed them for fear. English social feeling was not more re-assuring. It is unnecessary to dilate on the occurrences of 1774, when Wilkes was elected Lord Mayor and returned for Middlesex, to illustrate the then temper or tone of political parties. Dissatisfaction thereby aroused had become chronic. The Gordon

Riots of 1780 declare the later state of the public mind. In the provinces an universal outcry against Arkwrights' machinery had led to most formidable combinations of the working classes, who believed labour would cease if such facilities for production were permitted. In this condition of the public mind we have one important explanation of England's deficient energy when the necessity for action on Irish matters arose. There was another reason even more significant. England was in want both of money and of men. The American declaration demanded prompt action on the part of the Crown. The Irish establishment was ordinarily 12,000 strong. A requisition of 4,000 troops was made from Ireland, with a proposal that "for the better protection of that country, it was His Majesty's intention, if desired, to replace them by an equal number of Hessians (Protestants,)" adding that "their charge should be defrayed without expense to Ireland." The requisition was granted, but the protection of the foreign troops refused. It thus happened that when the Irish coast towns were threatened, their means of defence were not equal to the occasion. The requisition for Irish troops spoke in language which could not be misunderstood. Events progressed; "England's difficulty," as modern agitators are wont to assert, proved "Ireland's opportunity." It occurred thus: France by entering into a treaty of friendship and of commerce (4th July 1776), had assumed and recognised American Independence; ships of both nations together infested the Irish Channel; vessels trading between English and Irish ports were seized; a descent on the northern coast was apprehended. The inhabitants of Belfast appealed to England for help, but the Government was powerless for any such purpose. Permission was given to raise a volunteer corps for protection. Belfast at once did so, the Government providing the arms, and her example was followed by most of the northern towns. The command of Armagh was entrusted to the Earl of Charlemont, a nobleman who had established special claims to popularity by his successful advocacy of the rights of Irish Peeresses to be present at the Coronation. The Volunteer movement spread with astonishing rapidity and exercised an electric influence on all classes of the people. If may be safely affirmed that its progress and organization has no parallel in the history of nations. Armed associations sprang up in all directions, formidable alike from their number and their discipline. By their calm and determined attitude they commanded the respect without as yet awakening the apprehensions of England. Their presence nevertheless gave unmistakeable force to Irish remonstrance, and could not but exercise due influence on the deliberations of the British Cabinet. The Government, even if they so desired it, were without means of controlling the popular feeling. They had permitted the military power to pass out of the hands of the constituted authorities, and an armed force to spring into existence with which the regular troops were unable to cope. The natural and trusted leaders of the people were thereby placed in possession of the real power in the State. With its sense of strength, the nation was aroused to a desire for liberty, and insensibly assumed the high prerogative of demanding redress for grievances against which remonstrance had hitherto proved vain.

It is essential to inquire what those grievances were. In 1780, the political position of Ireland was one of complete dependence on Great Britain. Her Parliament at no time possessed real power, being in truth but the mouthpiece of the English minister. This condition was referable to the year 1495, when Henry VII., desirous to prevent a repetition of possible grievances from rival measures in dual Parliaments, sent Sir Edward Poynings to compose the distracted state of the English pale, and settle those differences which the contests of the Houses of York and Lancaster had occasioned. As King's deputy, he summoned a Parliament in Drogheda in the year stated, and passed the act known as "Poyning's Act," [App. 1.] which placed the initiation in the King's Lieutenant in Council, and required the sanction of the King in Council to all laws to be submitted to the Irish Parliament. In the third year of Philip and Mary its provisions were further extended by empowering " the Governor and Council to certify such other causes requiring legislation as were not foreseen at the beginning of the Session." It is unnecessary to elaborate the subsequent dependency of the Irish Parliament which, according to Campbell the historian of 1789, was little better than the registry of Royal edicts; nor is there occasion to follow it through the varying fortunes of its political existence, suspended or transferred as expediency or the whim of their rulers might suggest. It never was deprived of the privilege of the weak, to refuse to ratify that which it was powerless to resist; not that acceptance or refusal materially affected the ultimate result, and this for reasons which will be abundantly evident.

There had been some who ventured to think, that however Independent legislation was prevented, the laws of Ireland were free from control in their Irish administration. In this they were in error. It will be sufficient to quote the well-known statute 6 Geo. I, c. 5, [App. 2.] the very title of which—" An Act for better securing the dependency of Ireland upon the Crown of Great Britain," sufficiently illustrates the respective positions of their Parliaments, and the relations of their Courts of law. The facts which were considered to necessitate its enactment were simple. The Irish House of Lords reversed the decision of the Court of Exchequer. The plaintiff, one Sherlock, however, appealed further to the English House of Lords, which set aside the judgment of the Irish House. A conflict between both Houses ensued, which resulted in the Act under consideration. It declared that the Kingdom of Ireland was wholly subordinate to, and dependent on, the Crown of Great Britain; that the British Parliament had full power to enact laws to bind it; that all claim of appellate jurisdiction by the Irish House of Lords was unfounded, and all proceedings thereon null and void to all intents and purposes whatever. Thus doubly bound, first, in their incapacity to initiate laws which *de facto* they could carry to ultimate legislation, and secondly, in their inability to determine *de ure* legal appeals, the form of legislation was preserved, whilst the spirit of legislation was crushed. Matters of routine were unnoticed, on all others the English veto admitted of no appeal.

At intervals attempts had been made to exercise independent authority. Thus, in 1729, a majority succeeded against the Crown in limiting to yearly grants the Irish payments of national interest. Again, in 1751, the Commons asserted the principle of their right to dispose of the surplus of the hereditary revenue without the previous consent of the Crown. In 1769, they rejected money bills originated in the Privy Council. These, however, were occasions in which, without their action, the proceedings would have been incomplete. There is no instance where the Irish Parliament initiated and carried to completion any measure in opposition to the English Government. The student of history naturally seeks for some explanation as to the constitution of a Parliament that so represented a not inconsiderable nation.

The explanation rests on the surface—the vices of conquest had survived its memory. The Irish Parliament at no time represented the Irish people. The House of Peers was either dependent or expectant on the favour of the Crown, and powerless in the active business of the State. The House of Commons in its Borough representations, still, in 1780, fulfilled the purposes of their original formation:—to supply seats for creatures of the Crown. Of the 300 members, who at the time of the Union constituted the House of Commons, 200 were the nominees of individuals under the influence of the Government; forty, if not fifty, were returned by constituencies of ten persons, and several boroughs had no resident electors, some only one. It may be stated, on the authority of Henry Grattan, that two-thirds of the Representatives were returned by less than one hundred electors. Their election was also octennial. Unless influenced by a spirit of patriotism, the personal interests of members lay in inaction. Two-thirds of the intelligent life of Ireland were, because of their creed, without a voice in, or the means of influencing, her Councils. The penal acts were maintained in full rigour. It may be well to mention some of the principal disabilities under which the Roman Catholics rested at the commencement of these agitations. They could not hold leases for more than thirty-one years, could not purchase land, nor possess a horse of more than £5 value. They could not carry arms; they could not hold commissions in the army; they were specially excluded from the exercise of the franchise, and could not become barristers, six-clerks or attorneys, without taking the oaths of allegiance and supremacy. They could not hold any office under the Crown, or be created magistrates without taking the Sacrament as prescribed by the English Test Act, according to the usage of the Church of England. They could not inherit from Protestants by descent, nor bequest or devise. Upon death, their property divided. They could not intermarry without incurring penalties. Their educational privileges were restricted, and their business capacity also subject to rules, by which they were seriously fettered in the exercise of all civil or religious liberties.

The social condition of Ireland was what might have been expected from the constitution of its legislature. In a debate in the English House of Commons on the 10th of May 1776, the Hon. Temple Luttrell, speaking of the Irish, said that "a people so wretched, so oppressed, were scarcely to be found in any part of the civilised globe." Two years later, on the 16th of December, Lord Nugent in the British House of Commons described the people of Ireland "as suffering every species of misery and distress human nature was capable of bearing,—a people, nine-tenths of whom laboured for fourpence a day; whose food in summer was potatoes and buttermilk, and in winter potatoes and water."* Lord Beauchamp declared, in 1779, "that good estates in Ireland were offered for sale at sixteen and fourteen years' purchase, yet no buyers appeared at that low price." The only class that seemed indifferent was the Irish absentee, who drained his estate to its uttermost, and against whom law and remonstrance seemed equally unavailing. Then, as now, the Irish peasant adopted the aphorism of Bacon, that "revenge is a kind of wild justice." Certain it is, that he acted on that view. "The Right Boys" employed themselves in assailing the property of the Church; "The Levellors" in Munster resisted the enclosing of Commons by the levelling of fences and the houghing of cattle; "The Hearts of Oak" in Ulster were banded against the levying of land cess, and provisions for repair of roads; "The Hearts of Steel" in Leinster resisted the imposition of fines on the renewal of leases, and other, as they termed them, 'landlord exactions,' set forth in a petition to the Viceroy and published to the nation.† "The

---

* 1 Plowd. p. 118. † Froude vol. 2. p. 121.

Rockites" had Munster as their stronghold, though their members were generally diffused throughout the country. Captain Rock, their presumed leader, addressed his letters to the King, contending that no private rights should constitute or were consistent with public wrongs. To these might be added " Defenders " and " Peep o' day Boys," as illustrative of the pre-disposition of the Irish to combinations against the law, as well as in corroboration of the assertion that many social grievances demanding redress existed.

The condition of the manufacturing community was scarcely better. The journals of the Irish Commons abound with petitions from all kinds of Industries praying for State aid. The people were willing to transfer any faults which rested in themselves to their rulers. The writings of Molyneux, Swift and Lucas were the text books of an Irishman's political creed; these attributed any shortcomings to his inability to make the laws. The memories of such writers survived in their teachings, which bore fruit in the alacrity with which the Irish peasant ever entered into combinations promising successful resistance to English rule.

The year 1780 must ever be memorable in the history of Ireland. At its commencement the Volunteers were computed to number 30,000 men, self-equipped and strictly disciplined. To this force wealthy Roman Catholics had largely contributed, and in its ranks, notwithstanding laws to the contrary, were to be found not a few whose patriotism was for the time their highest creed and whose faith was complacently judged by that standard. In the Spring of the year a more extensive organisation of the force took place. The Earl of Charlemont, with Mr. Grattan as his aide-de-camp, assumed the position of leaders. Officers of Divisions were appointed. "Thus," says Plowden, "the foundation of the Irish Union was laid." With the confidence of authority which the support of an armed people gave, Mr. Grattan and his friends grew loud in their denunciations of what were conceived to be their country's wrong. The closer association of the rival sects, and the loyalty which Roman Catholics displayed, caused their grievances to be first considered. The Government did not deem it prudent to steadfastly resist their claims, and to Mr. Luke Gardiner was entrusted the introduction of Bills for their relief.

In the Session of 1778, the disabilities imposed by 2 Anne c. 6 and 8 Anne c. 3, were so far removed as to permit Papists to take leases for a term of 999 years, determinable on five lives, and to dispose by will or otherwise of land. Their estates were also rendered descendible, divisible and transferable, as if in seisin of any other. Conformity of eldest son was no longer to alter Papist parents' estate.* In Session of 1781-2, having taken the oath of allegiance, they were further entitled to take, hold, and dispose of lands in the same manner as Protestants, except Advowsons, Manors or Boroughs returning members to Parliament.† A third Act allowed persons professing the Popish religion to teach in schools, and repealed laws relating to the guardianship of their children, at the same time providing for their education.‡ Roman Catholics were thus restored to their rights of person, property and religion, and yet the distinction drawn by Flood, between the rights of property and the rights of power, had been carefully preserved. Nor were these the only indications of advancing toleration. Protestant dissenters were relieved from the Sacramental test before holding civil or military offices.|| Marriages between Protestant dissenters were permitted to be solemnized by dissenting clergymen.§ Many other vexatious observances were also dispensed with.

Having so far conciliated sects, the Volunteers took up the question of commerce. In consequence of numerous addresses from Ireland, a Committee had been appointed by the English Commons in 1778, to consider the Acts relating to Irish trade. It had reported thereon, and proposed to allow the exportation from Ireland to British plantations of all goods, wares and merchandise, with the exception of wool and woollens, and also a free import to Ireland of all merchandise from America, Africa and the West Indies. The measures were opposed by manufacturers in England, and the proposed Bills were abandoned. A motion by Lord Shelburne on the subject was negatived by a

---

* 17 and 18 Geo. III. c. 24. † 21 and 22 Geo. III. c. 24.
‡ 21 and 22 Geo. III. c. 62. || 19 and 20 Geo. III. c. 6.
§ 21 and 22 Geo. III. c. 25.

majority of 61—30. The people of Ireland resented such policy. They formed associations against the import of British commodities, and resolved to encourage and consume native manufactures only. When the House of Commons met in October, 1779, Mr. Grattan moved an amendment to the address, which was agreed to as follows :—" That we beg leave, however humbly, to represent to His Majesty that it is not by temporary expedients, but by a free trade alone that this nation is now to be saved from impending ruin." They at the same time resolved, by a majority of 170—47, that it would be inexpedient to grant new taxes, and they determined to pass but a six months' money Bill. The manner in which these resolutions were carried was significant. Care was taken that the Volunteers should be associated with the measures. Thanks were voted to them for their spirited defence of the Kingdom, the Prime Sergeant, Mr. Hussey Burgh, observing, " The British Ministers had lost one empire by their ignorance and weakness, and had here almost lost another ;" adding, " a short money Bill and a resolute people would make them insist on free trade ;" and concluding, " The English have sowed their laws like serpents' teeth, and they have sprung up in armed men." The Minister had no alternative but to accept what was offered. The resolutions induced Lord North to bring in his Bill for free trade to the British plantations, and it received the Royal assent before the recess.

Encouraged by such success, the Volunteers became loud in their demands for further concessions. The newspapers, their organs, declared "that Ireland was an Independent Kingdom, entitled to all the uncontrolled rights and immunities attaching thereto." These sentiments found an echo throughout the land, and Mr. Grattan, on the meeting of Parliament, moved in a full House, that " The King's most excellent Majesty and the Lords and Commons of Ireland, are the only power competent to make laws to bind Ireland." * The debate on his motion rivalled those of the present day ; the division took place at six o'clock in the morning, when the motion was lost by 133—99. In no wise dismayed by defeat,

* April 19th, 1780.

Mr. Grattan continued to declaim on the wrongs of Ireland. A want of appreciation of the situation was evident on the part of the Crown. A Mutiny Bill sent over, was returned by the English Privy Council altered, by being made perpetual. A Bill relating to sugar was also changed by imposing duty on lump, so as seriously to affect the Irish trade. They were, notwithstanding, passed by the Irish Commons, with many of whom, even then, the inspirations of freedom were giving way to the corruptions of place. When the facts became known, petitions to Parliament against their provisions grew and multiplied, and the expressions of popular disapproval became loud and unceasing. Against the manifestation of public feeling the Government was powerless. Lord North had been advised of impending dangers. Lord Weymouth had written the Earl of Buckinghamshire to "prevent the people arming or assembling;" he was informed in reply, "It was too late." To interfere, there must be a British army, and there was not in the country 3,000 soldiers. Buckingham applied for money to arm the militia, and was told "there was none." Happy for both countries it was so; for in the then temper of the two nations, a conflict must have been inevitable. Be this as it may, between want of Ministerial resolution and want of money, the opportunity was lost, and henceforth the Government was entirely at the mercy of the Volunteers. The Session shortly afterwards terminated. The Earl of Buckinghamshire, in his speech at its close, expressed "his satisfaction at the conduct of Great Britain in removing restrictions of trade, and at the free and equal intercourse of Ireland in her trade with the Colonies." During the prorogation, the Earl of Carlisle was appointed Lord Lieutenant, with Mr. Eden as Secretary. Why they were selected it is difficult to conjecture; they had been the unsuccessful Commissioners to America, to try and arrange the existing grievances, wherein they not only most egregiously failed, but gave rise to much public scandal by their assumed sanction of the attempt of their colleague Johnstone to bribe Reed, aide-de-camp to Washington. They entered on their new duties at a period full of difficulty.

There is a class of questions "which cannot retrograde, cannot remain stationary, but which must needs go on." The Volunteer movement afforded an illustration. When Parliament met on the 9th of October, 1781, it did so in the presence of an armed nation. The demands of the Commons were not likely, under such circumstances, to be refused. On the 10th of October, Sir S. Bradstreet, the Recorder of Dublin, moved for leave to bring in the heads of a Habeas Corpus Act. In 1774, a similar motion had been held irreconcilable with the idea of a dependency, and notice was sent to the Irish Council to "transmit the bills no more." Mr. Eden,* the Secretary, now supported it and expressed his approval of a clause which provided for its suspension during rebellion or invasion. The Bill founded on this motion became law.† Though due to the efforts of Parliament before its Independence, it is worthy of remark that the second clause runs thus :—" To the end that no sheriff, gaoler, or other officer may pretend ignorance of the import of any such writ, be it enacted by the authority aforesaid That all such writs shall be marked in this manner—' by the Statute of the Twenty-second year of the reign of King George the Third,' and shall be signed by the person that awards the same."

On the same day leave was given " to bring in heads of a Bill for making the Commissions of the Judges of this Kingdom to continue " *quam diu se bene gesserint*," and that Mr. Forbes, Mr. George Ponsonby, Mr. Yelverton and Sir Samuel Bradstreet do prepare and bring in the same." On the 30th October, Mr. Forbes brought in the Bill, which was received, read, and committed, and on the 5th of November, a Committee of the whole House considered it. When Mr. Speaker resumed the chair, Mr. Forbes reported " That they had gone through the heads of the said Bill, paragraph by paragraph, without any amendment," and it was ordered " that Mr. Forbes do attend his Excellency the Lord Lieutenant with the said heads of a Bill, and desire that the same may be transmitted to Great Britain in due form." The Bill was transmitted. On the 4th February following, the Recorder moved " that the present salaries of the Judges are inadequate to

---

* 1 Par. Deb. p. 10.   † 21 and 22 Geo. III. c. 11.

the dignity of their station." Mr. Grattan then complained "that the Bill which had passed the House and was sent over to England, to render Judges independent of the Crown during good behaviour, had not been returned." On the 16th of April, when speaking to the House, Mr. Grattan observed, "A Judges' Bill he refrained from mentioning, as he had found it was returned.' The reason why it had not become law was given by the Chief Secretary on the 30th of May, when Mr. Forbes again moved for leave to introduce the Bill.* "A Bill had already been sent over to England for the purpose, but was altered, though he had an assurance from the noble Lord now at head of Council not done by him, but he found it altered, and afterwards, by the unaccountable mistake of the Clerk in confounding the transcript with report, it came over in that altered condition." This is sufficient to show that while the Parliament was yet dependent, this important concession had practically been obtained. It afterwards became law,† but not before the Independence was acknowledged.

The difference in the reception given to these measures, which had hitherto been rejected, was obvious. On the 11th of December, Mr. Flood moved that Poyning's Law be considered. The question was discussed, and leave refused by 139—67. Thereupon the influence of the Volunteer movement became more fully understood. On the 28th of December, 1781, a meeting was held at Armagh, of the Southern battalion of the Ulster Regiment of Volunteers, who passed resolutions expressive of their concern at the desertion of the Constitutional rights of the Kingdom by the Irish Parliament. They convened a general meeting of delegates from all the Volunteer Corps of Ulster to take place at Dungannon on the 15th of February following, "then and there to deliberate on the alarming state of public affairs, and to determine on and publish to their country what may be the result of said meeting." It was intimated that bold steps would be proposed. The concluding resolution was, "that as it is highly probable the idea of forming brigades will be agitated and considered, the several corps of Volunteers who send delegates to

---

* Par. Deb. p. 377.   † 21 and 22 Geo. III., c. 50.

said meeting are requested to vest in them a power to associate with some one of such brigades as may be there formed." This circular caused dismay at the Castle. The Viceroy consulted Lord Hillsborough as to how such a difficulty was to be overcome. He advised the use of secret service money. Eden replied " he could take no more from the Irish Treasury without accounting for it." There was therefore no course open but to submit.

The memorable day of meeting at length arrived. The representatives of the 143 Corps of Volunteers met in the church of Dungannon, and passed resolutions proclaiming their national, political and commercial independence and freedom. [App. 3.] These resolutions were signed by men of the highest station and influence in the Kingdom. An address was, at the same time, voted and sent to the minority of both Houses of Parliament, signed by order of the Chairman. It was as follows :—" My Lords and Gentlemen, We thank you for your noble and spirited, though hitherto ineffectual efforts, in defence of the great and commercial rights of your country. Go on ! The almost unanimous voice of the people is with you ; and, in a free country, the voice of the people must prevail. We know our duty to our Sovereign, and are loyal. We know our duty to ourselves, and are resolved to be free. We seek for our rights, and no more than our rights ; and in so just a pursuit we should doubt the being of a Providence if we doubted of success.—Signed by Order, William Irvine, Chairman."

In the following week, on the 22nd of February, Mr. Grattan moved in the House of Commons an address to His Majesty embodying the substance of the resolutions, declaratory of the legislative independence of Ireland, and repudiating the right of Great Britain to bind her by any law whatsoever. The motion was opposed by the Government. The Attorney-General raised fears about the disturbance of the Act of Settlement as affecting the tenure of lands, the debate was adjourned, and the motion lost by 137—68. Mr. Flood, in no wise dismayed, on the 26th of the same month, moved (26th February, 1782)—

1st. " That the members of this House are the only representatives of the people of Ireland.

2nd. "That the consent of the Commons is indispensably necessary to render any statute binding."

The Solicitor-General moved as an amendment that the words "It is not now necessary to declare," should be inserted before the words in the original resolution. A division took place with a similar result.

Meantime affairs in England had daily grown more serious. Lord North's administration tottered to its close. On the receipt of the news of the American disaster, which arrived two days before the opening of Parliament, he found it was impossible to longer hold office. On the 14th day of March the Irish Parliament was adjourned to the 16th of April. Lord North resigned on the 20th of March. He regarded the matter as of little moment. The Earl of Surrey had given notice of a hostile motion. North knew resistance was hopeless, and being desirous to avoid discussion which might damage his friends, he was present at the opening of the House. He and Surrey rose together. Fox moved that the Earl of Surrey be heard. Lord North spoke to the motion, and announced his resignation. The anticipated debate did not come off. The majority of the members had ordered their carriages for a late hour. Heavy snow was falling. The Opposition, and many of his past friends who had joined them, stood shivering as North passed to his carriage. Before driving off, he looked at them, and observed, "Good night, gentlemen! you see the advantage of being in the secret."

On the resignation of Lord North the King sent for Lord Shelburne, and empowered him to form an administration. The Earl went to the Marquis of Rockingham, and offered him the Treasury and Premiership. "My Lord," he said, "you could stand without me. I cannot stand without you." The offered positions were accepted, and Lord Shelburne and Mr. Fox became principal Secretaries. Sixteen years had elapsed since the Marquis of Rockingham, without an adverse vote, had been dismissed from the same high offices, because of his running counter to the prejudices of the King. While out of office he had offered a strenuous, though ineffective, opposition to arbitrary and unwise measures, whose calamities he had foreseen, but the enactment of which he was powerless to prevent. His previous administration, though short lived, had been not unfruitful in great events, by which he had gained high character for statesmanship and fair dealing. The distractions of the British Empire had been composed, obnoxious taxation repealed, the House of Commons had passed resolutions condemning the use of general warrants and the seizure of papers in cases of libel. It was the time when Grenville's Stamp Act was laying the foundation of the American revolt. The Minister recognised the gravity of the situation. He determined to repeal the measure, and at the same time, in order to conciliate the King, to declare that the power of Parliament over the colonies was supreme. The feelings of the King were violently opposed to such a concession. The first Pitt, by very lavish promises and very earnest solicitation of the King, was induced to say that should a vacancy arise he would again enter his service ; the Marquis of Rockingham was thereupon dismissed, after office of one year and twenty days. Edmund Burke, whom he had as private secretary, wrote "a short account" of the administration, in which he observed : " They practised no corruption, nor were they even suspected of it. They sold no office. They obtained no reversions or pensions, either coming in or going out, for themselves, their families or dependents." His new Ministry had Edmund Burke as Paymaster of the Forces, and Richard Brinsley Sheridan as Under-Secretary of State. From such a Premier, so supported, the Irish nation had grounds to expect much. No appointment could have raised higher hopes. The Duke of Portland was named as Lord-Lieutenant of Ireland. Of him Walpole observed, " Until nominated to that office one hundred men were not aware of his existence." He entered on his duties with full knowledge of the social and political condition of the country. The return to London of Lord Carlisle, and of his secretary, Mr. Eden, placed the Ministry in possession of the actual state of Irish affairs. So impressed was Mr. Eden with the urgency of the situation that, on the 8th of April, 1782, he moved in the English House of Commons a repeal of the declaratory Act of 6 Geo. I., so far as it asserted a right in the King and Parliament of Great Britain to bind Ireland. He assured the

House " delays were useless, for in the present state and disposition of Ireland, they might as well strive to make the Thames flow up Highgate Hill as attempt to legislate for Ireland, which would no longer submit to any legislature but its own." Mr. Fox asked, on the part of the new Ministry, an adjournment till the next day : a Council was at once held, and the following message communicated to the English Parliament as its result :—" George R. His Majesty, being concerned to find that discontent and jealousies are prevailing amongst his loyal subjects in Ireland upon matters of great weight and importance, earnestly recommends to this House to take the same into their most serious consideration in order to such a final adjustment as may give mutual satisfaction to both kingdoms." The House resolved, *nem. con.*, " That an humble address be presented to His Majesty, to return His Majesty the thanks of this House for his most gracious message ; and to assure His Majesty that this House, feeling with His Majesty the deepest concern that discontents and jealousies should have arisen amongst His Majesty's loyal subjects in Ireland will, without delay, take the same into their most serious consideration, in order to such a final adjustment as may give mutual satisfaction to both Kingdoms."

On the 14th of April the Duke of Portland arrived in Dublin ; his entry was greeted with every demonstration of satisfaction. On the 16th, the Parliament of Ireland met. The Duke went in state, and in a speech to both Houses communicated the Royal Message and a suitable resolution was passed in the House of Peers [App. 4.] In the Commons, when Mr. John Healy Hutchinson brought forward a similar resolution, a notice of which he had entered on the minutes, Mr. Grattan moved that it be expunged, and in its stead proposed an amendment, which claimed :—

1st. The repeal of the Perpetual Mutiny Bill, and the dependency of the Irish army on the Irish Parliament.

2nd. The abolition of the legislative powers of the Council.

3rd. The abrogation of the claim of England to make law for Ireland.

C

4th. The exclusion of the English House of Peers, and of the English King's Bench, from any judicial authority in this realm.

5th. The restoration of the Irish Peers to their final judicature. The independence of the Irish Parliament in its sole and exclusive legislature.

His concluding words were, "These are my terms ; I will take nothing from the Crown," [App. 5.]

The two addresses, as resolved by the Lords and Commons, were presented by Mr. Secretary Fox to the British House of Commons, on May 1st, 1782. It is worthy of remark that in Mr. Grattan's elaborate resolution no mention is made of the Catholic question as being either a "grievance" or "a just cause of discontent or jealousy."

On the 14th of May the House adjourned for three weeks, in order to give the British Parliament time to take into consideration the claims made by Ireland. On the 17th of the same month, the Earl of Shelburne in the Peers, and Mr. Fox in the Commons, brought forward the subject of the Irish addresses. Mr. Fox moved "that it is the opinion of this Committee (a Committee of the whole House) that the Act of the 6th Geo. I. ought to be repealed ;" he declared, "it was downright tyranny to make laws for the internal Government of a country who were not represented amongst those by whom such laws were made." "If," said Fox, "I make a proposition hurtful to the pride of Englishmen, the fault is not mine. It is the fault of those who left it in the power of the Volunteers to make the demands, who left it in their power, not by leaving arms in their hands, but by leaving them injuries and oppressions." The proposal was unanimously adopted, and Mr. Powis reported two resolutions :—

1. That the Act of Geo. I. ought to be repealed.

2. That it is indispensable to the interest and happiness of both Kingdoms that the connexion between them should be established by mutual consent, upon a solid and permanent basis."

A Bill to repeal the obnoxious Act was ordered, and an address to the Crown in the terms of the second resolution.

The terms in which the Duke of Portland conveyed the Royal

assent to the Irish claim were flattering. On the 27th of May, in his speech, he said, " It gives me the utmost satisfaction that the first time I have occasion to address you, I find myself enabled by the magnanimity of the King and the wisdom of the Parliament of Great Britain, to assure you that immediate attention has been paid to your representations, and that the British legislature have concurred in a resolution to remove the causes of your discontents and jealousies, and are united in a desire to gratify every wish expressed in your late addresses to the throne."

"These benevolent intentions of His Majesty, and the willingness of his Parliament of Great Britain to second his gracious purposes, are unaccompanied by any stipulation or condition whatever. The good faith, the generosity, the honour of this nation, afford them the surest pledge of a corresponding disposition on your part, to promote and perpetuate the harmony, the stability and the glory of the Empire."

The day following His Majesty's answer to the address was itself laid on the table, and on the same day a reply was agreed on. Its material parts were as follow:—

" To assure His Majesty that we conceive the resolution of an unqualified, unconditional repeal of the 6th of George the First to be a measure of consummate wisdom and justice, suitable to the dignity and eminence of both nations, exalting the character of both, and furnishing a perpetual pledge of mutual amity.

"That gratified in these particulars, we do assure His Majesty that no constitutional question between the two nations will any longer exist, which can interrupt their harmony ; and that Great Britain, as she has approved of our firmness, so may she rely on our affection.

"That we remember, and do repeat our determination to stand and fall with the British nation."

On the 29th of May, there was appointed a day of General Thanksgiving, "To return thanks for the many blessings bestowed on the Kingdom of Great Britain and Ireland, and particularly for that union, harmony, and cordial affection which has been happily brought about between these two Kingdoms, whose interests are inseparably the same, by the wisdom and justice of

His Majesty and his Councils in forming and re-establishing their mutual rights, by which the strength, honour, happiness and glory of the whole Empire are greatly augmented; and for the great success of His Majesty's arms against our natural enemies, which we trust will bring about a happy, stable, and lasting general peace to these Kingdoms."* On the 30th the House resolved itself into a Committee of the whole House to take into consideration " what sum of money it may be proper to grant for the purpose of purchasing an estate and building a mansion to be settled on Henry Grattan, in testimony of our gratitude for the unequalled services he has done this Kingdom." A sum of £100,000 was proposed, which at Mr. Grattan's own request was reduced to £50,000. Mr. Conolly then stated,† " He was happy to inform the House, that the Lord Lieutenant did most perfectly coincide in their generous intentions, so congenial to his own feelings; and that the memory of such great events might be perpetuated, he wished to relinquish to the object of the nation's esteem that house in the Park which Parliament had lately purchased for the country residence of His Majesty's representative. This House, properly furnished, with an annuity of £2,500 a year, would be a handsome thing and less burdensome to the nation than the £50,000 proposed," —a mark of appreciation which contrasts strangely with the fact, that Mr. Flood, who in 1781 resigned the most lucrative post in the gift of the Crown because he disapproved of the policy then followed, and co-operated with Mr. Grattan, had been removed from the list of the Privy Council by Lord North, and was not restored to honour on this day of General Thanksgiving.

An address to the Duke of Portland followed, in which he was assured that " these are not the trite expressions of mere formal duty, but the pure effusions of genuine gratitude from a free people to a chief Governor, who has announced from the throne the ratification of their freedom, descended from a line of constitutional ancestors, inheriting their principles with their blood." They added, that " we cannot but rejoice that the name of Bentinck, so intimately connected with the great era of British liberty, will be handed

* Com. Jour. 29th May, 1782. † P. Deb. vol. 1, 379.

down to the latest posterity, inseparably blended with the full and perfect establishment of the Constitution of Ireland."

Having thus exhausted congratulations and, in the intoxication of success, discovered in each other the most splendid virtues, and vowed eternal friendship with Great Britain, the Irish Parliament put its hand into the Exchequer and voted £100,000 for raising men for the fleet. Mr. Yelverton the same day brought in a Bill to repeal Poyning's Law, whilst in the British House of Commons the 6th of George I. was repealed. [App. 6.] Mr. Flood contended that the mere repeal of a declaratory act fell short of the requirements of the occasion. There were but two modes of dealing with the difficulty; the one, by a renunciation of what England held to be right, but which it was ready to give up, and which, however, it was foreseen might give offence to the people of Ireland, who contended that England never had such right; the other by declaring that England, though she had exercised, had never been legally possessed of such right. To this latter mode it was justly apprehended that the Parliament of Great Britain would not be brought to consent, and Mr. Fox therefore adopted simple repeal as most consistent with the spirit of the people of Ireland, and the dignity of the English Parliament.*

Mr. Flood brought his opinions before the House on the 19th of July, contending that the mere repeal of a declaratory law did not affect the principle, and moved "That leave be given to bring in heads of a Bill for declaring the sole and exclusive right of the Irish Parliament to make laws in all cases whatever, internal and external, for the Kingdom of Ireland;" a motion which was negatived without a division. Mr. Grattan thereupon protested "That leave was refused to bring in said heads of a Bill because the sole and exclusive right of legislation in the Irish Parliament, in all cases, whether internally or externally, hath been already asserted by Ireland, and fully, finally, and irrevocably acknowledged by the British Parliament," which was adopted without division.

* "Memoirs of Right Hon. Henry Flood." Dublin, 1838, p. 160.

While these public expressions of mutual confidence were being exchanged, we are permitted to refer to a correspondence which throws much light on the matter, and which twenty years later was printed by order of the English Parliament. It is the official correspondence between the Duke of Portland, Lord Lieutenant of Ireland, and Lord Shelburne and others. [App. 7.] The importance of this correspondence cannot be over-estimated; it places beyond question the fact that efforts were even then being made to arrange the terms of a Union between the two countries, and that every influence within Parliament and outside of it was being suborned for that purpose. It appears to afford an explanation of the hopes and intentions of English Statesmen in their subsequent dealing with Irish Parliamentary votes. To carry through the proposed Union, Ministerial ascendency in Irish Councils was indispensable, and throughout the whole period of so-called Independence it was steadily maintained. How far it exercised an influence on debates and determined divisions will be apparent when the proper time for such considerations arises.

With this correspondence fresh in memory the Duke of Portland terminated the proceedings by a speech of congratulation and advice ; he observed, " You have provided for the impartial and unbiassed administration of justice by the Act for securing the independency of the judges ; you have adopted one of the most effectual securities of British freedom by limiting the Mutiny Act in point of duration ; you have secured the most invaluable of all human blessings, the personal liberty of the subject, by passing the Habeas Corpus Act ; you have cherished and enlarged the wise principles of toleration, and made considerable advances in abolishing those distinctions which have too long impeded the progress of industry, and divided the nation.

" Many and great national objects must present themselves to your consideration during the recess from Parliamentary business ; but what I would most earnestly press upon you, as that upon which your domestic peace and happiness, and the prosperity of the Empire at this moment most immediately depends, is to cultivate and diffuse those sentiments of affection and confidence, which are now happily restored between the two kingdoms. Convince the people in your several districts, as you are yourselves convinced, that every cause of past jealousies and discontents is finally removed ; that both countries have pledged their good faith to each other, and that their best security will be an inviolable adherence to that compact ; that the implicit reliance which Great Britain has reposed on the honour, generosity and candour of Ireland, engages your national character to a return of sentiments equally liberal and enlarged ; convince them that the two kingdoms are now one, indissolubly connected in unity of constitution and unity of interests, that the danger and security, the prosperity and calamity of the one must equally affect the other, that they stand and fall together."

Thus was Irish independence battled for and won ! How much of real liberty was thereby conferred ? What did this Irish enthusiasm signify ? Did it represent the active spirit of a free people, wise to conceive, and powerful to enact laws ? Or was it but the idol of an hour, which the popular will set up, and before which the multitudes bowed down ? Had it, as the image of old, a glittering head and feet of clay ? Did it, or did it not, prove equal to the responsibilities of Government ? These are grave questions. On their answers must depend the judgment of posterity.

ON the termination of the Rockingham administration the Irish Parliament was dissolved. A new Ministry, with the Earl of Shelburne as Premier, and William Pitt as Chancellor of the Exchequer, undertook the duties of office under circumstances of no ordinary difficulty. The association between Shelburne and Fox in one ministry, and Shelburne and Pitt in another, was significant. Earl Temple became the first Lord Lieutenant of Independent Ireland ; his appointment was considered an appropriate one, as he had married the daughter of Earl Nugent, and thereby acquired large Irish estates. The most that can be said of his administration is, that he was passive for the few months of his residence, and not having been called on for active duties he had no opportunity of making enemies. Before the Parliament re-assembled, another administration was formed. The English Commons had, in the interim, passed what was practically a vote of censure on the Government, by their resolutions in reference to the peace then concluded ; imputing that England had given to the American States too large concessions, and made inadequate provision for the security and indemnity of the loyalists. The influence of Lord North was too powerful for successful resistance ; and there was no alternative but resignation. The Duke of Portland became Premier ; Lord North, Fox, and the Earl of Carlisle members of his cabinet, whilst the Earl of Northington replaced Earl Temple. There was in the cabinet no want of knowledge on Irish affairs. On the 14th of October, 1783, the first Irish Independent Parliament met, and elected, without opposition, the Right Hon. Edmund Sexton Perry as their Speaker.

Lord Northington, in his speech from the throne, observed, "It is with more than ordinary satisfaction that, in obedience to His Majesty's commands, I meet you in full possession and enjoyment of those constitutional and commercial advantages which have been so firmly established in your last Parliament." He proceeded in the usual terms, and added, " The establishment of public tranquillity is peculiarly favourable at this period, and will naturally give spirit and effect to your commercial pursuits. Both kingdoms are now enabled to deliberate with undivided attention on the surest means of increasing their prosperity and reaping the certain fruits of reciprocal affection." There was nothing then to prevent the Duke of Portland from giving full and dispassionate consideration to Irish affairs. The ordinary topics—Linen Manufacture, Fisheries, Protestant Charter Schools, with the addition of Admiralty Laws—were recommended for consideration. An address in reply was voted ; it was then proposed, *nem. con.*, " That the thanks of the House be given to the Volunteers for their spirited endeavours to provide for the protection of their country, and for their ready and frequent assistance of the civil magistrates in enforcing the due execution of the laws." From this it may be inferred that the Volunteers had been practically accepted as part of the duly constituted forces of the country.

Before proceeding to examine how far the "peculiarly favourable" opportunity was used by the Independent Parliament, it is well to briefly review what had been accomplished by its predecessor.

The second Octennial Parliament may fairly be considered as most memorable in Irish history. Its members called into life the Volunteers, and its councils drew strength, if not inspiration, from the presence of an armed nation. While yet dependent, they loosened the chains of religious thraldom from the Roman Catholics ; they removed vexatious restrictions and observances from Protestant dissenters and those of similar creeds ; they secured the liberty of the subject by the Habeas Corpus Act ; they rendered the Judges independent of the Crown ; they acquired as much free trade for Ireland as she ever possessed ; they established the principle of a limited Mutiny Bill ; they vindicated their complete control over the Irish Exchequer. These are things worthy to be remembered, for they were accomplished in defiance of statutes which they repudiated and repealed. Had they, in addition, by International commissioners—as the correspondence of the Duke of Portland suggested—settled, for the then time, commercial questions and secured to their successors independence of action by means of a thorough Reform Bill, this, the Patriot Parliament, would have been without a rival in the political history of any country. In these omissions, opportunities were suffered to pass, which never, in the same form, were again presented.

The distress of the country had been great, in consequence of the American war necessitating restrictions upon trade, and imposing for two years an embargo on the Irish ports. Bad harvests, failure of the potato crops, and diminished tillage, conduced to further suffering. The last Parliament had carried the nation through a period in every sense exceptional, exercising on the English Government the constitutional force of public opinion, which, backed by arms, proved in this instance irresistible; proclaiming, as it did, that if redress was withheld a revolution was more than possible.

It might have been anticipated that with the Duke of Portland as Premier, his chief Governor of Ireland would have suggested the final adjustment of these commercial questions involving jealousies and discontents, which occupied the attention of previous Parliaments. He did not do so, and it may be because the public mind had in the meantime been diverted from the question. A General Election brings to the front the most pressing popular grievances. Peace had been proclaimed, there was a consequent reaction in trade. The burdens of taxation pressed heavily on the people. The national expenditure and the causes which conduced to it, naturally came under consideration. On the 28th of October, a motion of Sir Henry Cavendish was directed in general terms to the necessity of all practical retrenchments. This was by Mr. Flood especially pointed to the reduction of the army. Mr. Grattan spoke in opposition. Their personal and parliamentary encounter is familiar to all. The antagonism of these two great leaders, affords the probable explanation of the abortive action of the Session. The motion was postponed by 111—57. It may be stated that the Irish military establishment had been quietly restored to its full complement of 15,000 men. Against this, Mr. Flood moved an address on the 3rd of November, stating the expenses of the country to be excessive, and asking for a reduction of the army. Mr. Grattan opposed; his chief argument being the increased prosperity of Ireland in consequence of increasing trade and the removal of restrictions. A majority of 190—74 rejected the motion, and other motions of a similar character were also attempted, and met with a like result. The House of Lords deserves a passing notice for their rejection of money Bills, accompanied by conditions. They passed two resolutions expressive of their views.* [App. 8.] When the Bills thus returned reached the House of Commons, Mr. Curran declared the resolutions to be "an insult and an injury to the House," and moved "that it is the sole and undoubted privilege of the Commons of Ireland to originate all Bills of supply and grants of public money, in such manner and with such clauses as they shall think proper." The Irish Commons were not altogether unmindful of English precedents, and rejected the motion by 58—11.

Mr. Flood's doubts respecting the adequacy of "Simple Repeal" of Poyning's Act now received confirmation. It was said that Lord Mansfield had given judgment in an Irish case. The public were incensed, and, as was usual, strong expressions were used. Colonel Fitzpatrick had called attention to a decision of the English Court of King's Bench, as having given alarm in Ireland. Mr. Secretary Townsend explained that the cause had been before the Court for eighteen months, and that the judges were bound to decide it. He declared that the case stood alone ; that two cases pending before the English House of Lords had been sent back to Ireland, and that immediate steps would be taken by the English Parliament to render any further occurrence of the same kind impossible. Such an Act as that originally suggested by Mr. Flood was introduced in the English Parliament, and at once passed into law.† In its discussion in the Lords the Duke of

* Lord's Jour. p. 409.   † 23rd Geo. 3 c. 28.

Richmond observed, " all those arguments powerfully bore upon the ultimate necessity of an incorporate Union, without which the two kingdoms must be constantly exposed to monstrous anomalies and mischiefs in Government."

The General Election had brought prominently forward the abuses in the system of representation. Numerous petitions were presented for Parliamentary Reform. A petition from the County Tyrone is a fair example of the public feeling.* The petitioners " beg leave to suggest it as a doctrine not to be disputed that, agreeable to the Constitution, they, as freeholders, have a right to be adequately represented in the House, and the petitioners humbly trust that the House will be pleased to consider that the manner in which the House of Commons is at present constituted puts it out of the power, even of credulity itself to think, or sophistry to plead, that it is an adequate representation of the people." They proceeded : " indigent boroughs, nearly destitute of inhabitants, send members ; that in some boroughs no electors reside ; that in others rights of suffrage have been circumscribed or extended for individual purposes ; that Peers and Commoners have absolute nomination."

To ask for Parliamentary Reform was to ask many members to surrender their birthrights or to part with property they had dearly purchased, as well as to give up that political influence which was the source of their power. It was not likely they would do so. It was not to be expected that the Government would support a measure that might deprive them of the venal majority at their command. The few patriots of the Flood and Grattan type were as nothing in an assembly whose tenure rested on the anomalies complained of. True it was, when Mr. Flood, after repeated defeats, carried his Octennial Bill (1768), members who had opposed it found that, far from rendering their influence less, on the following election it afforded them an opportunity for exacting terms. The value of their property increased with the returning exercise of their influence. Mr. Flood recognised the difficulty in the way of further reform. It was a question to

* Common's Journals, vol. ii., p. 249.

be settled by the public opinion of the nation, and through the pressure thus brought to bear on Parliament. The Volunteer organization throughout the country presented to his view a machinery available for the purpose, and the Volunteers, who felt their influence waning, at once adopted the cry. A second "Convention," for the purposes of Parliamentary Reform was determined on, to be held at Dungannon on the 8th of September. Addresses were published throughout the country, in which the Volunteers did not fail to place their light upon a hill. They declared "that the Imperial Crown of Ireland had been restored by their efforts to its original splendour, and the nation to its inherent rights as an Independent State." They alleged "that the distracted inhabitants had been united in an indissoluble bond through an unparallelled combination of the civil and military authority," and they avowed "their determination to abolish the courtly mercenaries who preyed on the vitals of public virtue." Parliament thus forewarned was forearmed.

A Reform Convention, composed of 270 delegates from companies of Volunteers, met on the day appointed. Three resolutions were passed :—1. Freedom is the indefeasible right of Irishmen and Britons, derived from the Author of their beings, of which no power on earth has a right to deprive them. 2. Those only are free who are governed by no laws but those to which they assent, either in person or by their representatives freely chosen. 3. The elective franchise shall extend to those, and to those only, who will exercise it for the public good."

These political doctrines were but a feeble reflex of opinions in France, then arousing the world to arms. The third resolution was believed to include the other two, and so formed the justification to those members who resisted Reform ; for each one was ready to contend, that in his own return, the elective franchise had been admirably exercised. The Dungannon delegates determined on a Reform Bill, and agreed that a Convention should be held in Dublin ; they urged a renewal of that policy which had been previously successfully pursued. In this they reckoned without their host, and for this reason :—the ends to be accomplished and the interests to be assailed were now different.

The Government and the Parliament, on the question of Independence, had been opposed — the Government and the Parliament, in the maintenance of Parliamentary authority, had a common interest. When Independence was carried, the Volunteers were masters of the situation; now England's hands were untied, and her military forces free. The occasion offered itself to the executive by the successful resistance of this new action on the part of the Volunteers, to prepare the way for their discomfiture and downfall. Such, however, could only be accomplished by constitutional means, and Flood, in the course he pursued, afforded the opportunity. The Volunteer delegates to the number of 300, the same number as the Parliament, on the 10th of November, assembled in the Rotunda; their ranks included Peers and Commoners of high distinction; they assumed the functions of Parliament and prepared a plan of Reform, chiefly with the assistance of Mr. Flood; they sat continuously till the 29th of the same month. On that day Mr. Flood moved to bring in his Bill. [App. 9.] The House was crowded, the uniforms of the Volunteer members being especially conspicuous. It was rumoured amongst the members that Mr. Pitt was in favour of the Bill, and the proposed admission of Catholics to the franchise. The latter, however, formed no part of Mr. Flood's scheme, but, had the measure received full discussion, strong efforts would have been made on their behalf. It became a trial of strength between the Government and the Convention. The defeat of the measure was therefore of the first importance. To this end all the State influence had been directed. It was alleged that any Reform including Catholic representation would, from their numerical majority, lead to their ascendancy and a review by them of the Act of Settlement. The Catholic delegates were assured by what, in more modern times, would have been termed, "an impudent fabrication," that their Bishops and spiritual leaders were unfavourable to the scheme. Flattered or defied, as occasion required, the members of the Convention and the members of Parliament were pitted against each other; whilst the latter, conciliated by the personal influence of the Viceroy, or made safe by the more practical arguments of his Secretary, were prepared to admit the principle of Reform, but to vote against the introductiion of the Bill. This not a few did. The Attorney General opposed it on grounds which were far better than arguments ;—appeals to the pride and independence of the new Parliament, sitting in their first Session for the discharge of their duties ; " were they to be considered as unequal to their trusts ?" The measure was described by him as " the mandate of a military Congress." Flood and his allies were answered by ridicule, and treated with contempt. Mr. Grattan supported the motion for Reform in a few words of general approval of the principle, but without in any way committing himself to the plan introduced. The motion was lost by 158—49. The defeat of the Convention sounded the requiem of the political power of the Volunteers. While Parliament was still flushed by its sense of Independence in the rejection of this measure on grounds strangely similar to those by which its claims to Independence had been secured, the Attorney General moved, " that it is now become indispensably necessary to declare that the House will maintain its just rights and privileges against all encroachments whatsoever." This was carried by 150—68. Mr. Conolly then moved, "That an humble address be presented to His Majesty, to declare the perfect satisfaction which we feel in the many blessings we enjoy under His Majesty's most auspicious Government, and our present happy Constitution, and to acquaint His Majesty that at this time we think it peculiarly incumbent upon us to express our determined resolution to support the same inviolate with our lives and fortunes." A motion considered by Mr. Grattan to be unnecessary, and opposed by him without success.

In this condition of the Parliamentary mind, Mr. Molyneux (5th December 1783), moved to introduce an Absentee Tax [App. 11] of four shillings in the pound, on all rents remitted out of the Kingdom to non-resident landowners. The same old arguments were used which had on former occasions defeated the Bill. It was urged that the value of land would be lowered by such a tax, and the happy union so recently inaugurated between the two countries, and as yet on its trial, be interrupted. Sir John Blaquire, who had been Secretary in Lord Harcourt's Viceroyalty, reminded the

House of the circumstances under which the measure had been then introduced and lost. The Attorney General, not to appear indifferent, when the question as amended was put, moved that one shilling be substituted for four, as proposed ; it was lost by 184—22.

Again was Ireland to experience change. Another resignation of Ministers took place. The extraordinary coalition between North and Fox was brought to an ignominious close by the rejection of Fox's India Bill. So eminently distasteful was the measure to the King, that, when informed of the decision of Parliament, and the resignation of his Ministry, he ordered their seals of office to be delivered up to the new Secretaries of State, without a personal interview, "which would be disagreeable to His Majesty." Their dismissal was accepted by men of all ranks, parties and sects, without a murmur. The alliance had been regarded as an unnatural one. The public apprehended from it, to use the words of Wilberforce, " a progeny stamped with the features of both parents,—the violence of the one party and the corruption of the other." The Irish administration had, notwithstanding, been adroitly carried out. It was the most creditable feature of a political régime, which has since been quoted as an illustration, that " England does not love coalitions." On the dismissal of his Ministers the King sent for Temple. William Pitt became Premier. The Duke of Rutland was appointed to Ireland with Thomas Orde as his Chief Secretary.

Pitt's advent to office as Prime Minister inaugurated an administration which lasted throughout the remainder of the period under review. Heretofore short Ministries with undefined policies, and no confidence of continuing authority, had caused the office of Viceroy to be one far from desirable. The position was anomalous. The Irish Parliament claimed to be independent of English influence, if not alien from English sympathy. Its policy was, however, expected to adapt itself to the views of separate administrations, or be at variance with its Chief Governor. The inconvenience of such a system began to be publicly complained of ; nor were the complaints ill founded. Ministries were short lived, and changes were frequent. Lord Carlisle had admitted the Irish claims for Independence, pointing out to the English Minister the hopelessness of opposition ; he was removed before its attainment. The Duke of Portland sees in the adjustment of jealousies and differences the foundation of political and commercial union ; he leaves the questions unsettled. Earl Temple begins to understand his duties when his office terminates. The Earl of Northington recognises the antagonism of Irish parties, and in a crisis of great difficulty shows his appreciation of the position, when he is recalled. Is it then to be wondered at, that expediency, and not policy, governed a country whose councils in the hands of the Viceroy were chiefly available for the exigencies of the hour ?

As Nationalists affirm, the haste, " the fatal haste," of Grattan was herein evidenced. To his high-sounding resolution he sacrificed the opportunities afforded by the message of the King. The Irish claimed to be governed by the King, Lords, and Commons of Ireland, while the Royal assent to Irish Bills was provided to be given under the Great Seal of England. The Crown in all such cases is advised by the English Minister. By the Act of Renunciation the Great Seal had otherwise no authority in Ireland. The anomaly of the position is apparent ; since without the consent of the English Minister legislation was impossible. Had it been provided that the King of England as Sovereign of Ireland should be advised on Irish affairs by a Minister responsible to the Irish Parliament only, an Irish Cabinet with an Irish Viceroy, independent of English political changes, would have been the necessary result, and an abiding sense of responsibility might then have governed their councils. As it was, that responsibility perpetually shifted, and was not always equally understood. True ! whether as Sovereign of England or of Ireland, the advice of the Minister of England would have still prevailed with the King, whilst a fixed Viceroy and an independent Irish Cabinet would have reduced differences between the two nations to the alternative of separation or re-conquest. Where Irish measures were obnoxious, any middle course would then have been most difficult, as the English executive would have thereby surrendered the power and opportunity of "managing" Irish votes. It may be that Grattan, with far-seeing statesmanship, desired that English Ministerial influence should be still preserved; or, as was asserted, it may be that he failed to recognise the importance of the question. Whichever suggestion be true, fortunate indeed was the country that had still preserved to it such a way of ultimate escape from the bitter contention of sects and the turbulence of factions, as the Act of Union could alone afford.

The Duke of Rutland entered on office in a troublesome time. The question of reform had become the cry of the people, as the Volunteer Convention had proved a failure. Exasperated by their want of success, the Volunteers invited many Catholics to their ranks. Debarred from the exercise of the suffrage, the latter saw, in agitation, their sole hope of its ultimate attainment. The presence in the city of regular troops in considerable numbers, with the co-operation of the better-minded of the community, with difficulty preserved the peace. It demanded the utmost forbearance to prevent direct encounters between the mob and military; both the public tranquility and security were, at times, in imminent danger. The Lord-Lieutenant was not without sound advice. The Irish Privy Council was strong in the presence of Yelverton, Scott and Fitz-Gibbon, who had each afforded convincing proofs of their courage and knowledge in dealing with Irish affairs. Fitz-Gibbon was the ruling spirit of the Rutland Vice-regency. The arrival of the Lord-Lieutenant in February, 1784, found Ireland in a state of expectancy. It was the Interregnum of Reform. The question had been postponed, not decided. The English Minister was soon to learn the materials with which he had to deal. The members of either House of Parliament, who had influence to dispose of, flocked to the Chief Secretary.* The correspondence at the time discloses an amount of political mendicancy almost incredible. Orde writes, "he was almost distracted with the infinite numbers and variety of applicants for favour, who had all long stories to tell. The patronage of Ireland would not suffice for one day's short allowance for all who crowded into the ship to be fed."—Fitting comment on their rejection of reform!

* Froude, vol. ii., p. 396.

While avoiding direct conflict with the troops, every day afforded sad and unmistakeable evidence of the utter defiance of law or order which prevailed. Property was as insecure as life was unsafe. Mutilation and maiming were regarded as means of expressing political disapproval. For the restraint of the latter, special provision had to be made by an Act which, for all ages, must be a blot on the Irish Statute Book, as indicating the necessity of the times:—"An Act for the more effectual discovery and prosecution of offenders called houghers, and for the support and maintenance of soldiers and others houghed, maimed, and disabled by such offenders." [App. 12.] Houghing was the cutting of the *tendo Achilles*, and dividing the fibrous sheaths of the ham muscles, the victim being thereby disabled for life. In modern atrocities of semi-barbarous States history but repeats itself.

The Reform Agitation was again revived. Flood, on the defeat of his motion, had continued to agitate the question, and the Convention, on the rejection of their measure, had been induced to dissolve. The excuse of their dictation could no longer be urged in Parliament. Flood had carried over their addresses to the King. He obtained on his return leave to again introduce a Bill. He did so, and on the 4th of March it was fully and calmly discussed. Numerous petitions for reform had been presented,—their value was fully appreciated. Two classes of arguments were now urged by the opponents of the Bill. It was said, as the Catholics were excluded from its provisions, extension of the suffrage to Protestant leaseholders would lead to their replacing the Catholic tenantry; and unless provision was made to admit the Catholics, their hopes of future franchise would be at an end, and Protestant ascendancy perhaps lead to a withdrawal of the privileges which, after so many struggles, they had succeeded in obtaining. At the same time the Protestants were told they had before them demonstrative proof that their numerical inferiority would render political struggles hopeless should their religion cease to be a barrier to political freedom. These views found adherents in the turbulent crowds who clamoured for change, with the desperate hope that in the conflict of parties some practical good might result. Those who, uninfluenced by sectarian opinions, supported the Bill, had the stale arguments of existing abuses to be remedied. Grattan was called on to defend the Volunteers, who had been so active in reform agitation, from many imputations cast upon them; and, by so doing, recovered some of that popular favour he had partially forfeited. The argument which told best against the Bill was that which directly affected the interests of those whose seats were in danger if their influence was placed in jeopardy. On a division the Bill was lost by 159—85.

As was not unusual in Ireland, political disturbance was accompanied by great social distress. Tillage had been neglected for the sake of agitation; the character of the Volunteer movement had also undergone a marked change, its members had ceased to represent the sterling middle-class yeomen of the country, who had retired in large numbers when the Parliamentary Independence of Ireland was secured. They had been replaced by men of a very different type, who regarded an armed organization as the means of resisting the laws, rather than of upholding authority.

The operation of Free Trade had disappointed their expectations. Meetings were held in Dublin, at which addresses of all kinds were passed, imputing want of commercial faith to England. The refusal of Reform was also declared to be a denial of the rights of the people. The Constitution of 1782 was asserted to be a means whereby a venal House of Commons could always be brought within the influence of the Crown. Mr. Flood's last efforts on behalf of Reform were worse than his first. It was by his advice determined to revive agitation, and to summon a national Congress of 300 to deliberate on the course to be adopted. The North of Ireland, ever foremost in agitation, had in July conveyed a petition to Mr. Pitt for presentation to the King. Mr. Pitt replied "that he had undoubtedly been and still continued a zealous friend to a reform in Parliament, but that he must beg leave to say, that he had been so on grounds very different from those adopted in their petition. That what was there proposed he considered as tending to produce still greater evils than any of those which the friends of Reform were desirous to remedy."* Mr. Pitt was thereupon

* Plow, vol. ii.

denounced as false to his professions. The Corporation of Dublin took up the cry, and the High Sheriff called a meeting of the citizens on the 19th of August. Resolutions were proposed, which placed beyond doubt that even then were comedies copied from the French. [App. 13]. The Duke of Rutland proved equal to the occasion. He received the petition from the Dublin Corporation, complaining of the rejection of the Reform Bill; alleging many grievances, and asking for "a complete abolition of the penal laws oppressing Roman Catholics." The Duke agreed to transmit the address to the King, and added, " he should not fail to convey his entire disapprobation of it, as casting unjust reflections on the laws and Parliament of Ireland, and as tending to weaken the authority of both." In no wise intimidated by the answer of the Viceroy, the Sheriff threatened renewed agitation, but the matter was not suffered to proceed ; the High Sheriff was attached, the Attorney-General himself directing the proceedings. He was brought before the Kings' Bench, and sentenced to fine and imprisonment ; after a few days he was liberated, and the fine was reduced on his acknowledging his error, and making a public apology in Court.* Thus not only was the Law vindicated, but agitators were instructed as to the power of the Crown. The matter, however, was not suffered to rest; Mr. Brownlow gave notice of his intention to move for a Committee, but was absent when his motion came on. Lord Charles Fitzgerald moved, "the action of the Attorney-General was contrary to the principle of the Constitution as depriving the Sheriff of his trial by jury, and a precedent of a dangerous tendency." The Attorney-General declared, "that the Sheriff Henry Steevens Reilly had summoned the power of his county for the purpose of electing five persons as delegates to a National Congress, and had pledged the lives and fortunes of himself and of the power of his county, to support any and whatever alterations the said Congress should think proper to propose for a Reform of the Constitution,"—and concluded, "Now, Sir, on this ground I did attach him, and on this ground I am ready to defend what I have done." The Motion was put and lost by 143—71.

* Plowden, vol. ii.

While the Sheriff in Dublin was being thus dealt with, there had been no delay in warning the sheriffs throughout the different counties of the views of the Government, and notwithstanding outrage and tumult in Dublin, the schemes of the disaffected were baffled by the firmness of the executive, and especially of the Law Officers of the Crown, with the warm approval and support of Parliament. Mr. Pitt quite understood the difficulty, and approved of the course adopted. Mr. Pitt was known to be in favour of an English Reform Bill. It was his discussion of that question which had first secured to him public attention, and it was believed that as soon as he was more firmly seated in his administration, Reform of the English Parliament would be undertaken. The opinion was encouraged that a simultaneous Bill would be made an Irish measure with the assistance of the Crown, and that existing abuses would then receive their full measure of consideration. The seed thus sown produced good fruit. The more moderate of the Irish party were content to wait,—the more violent the Law was adequate to deal with.

There was little else of interest to prolong the Session.

Having promised so much and accomplished so little, Parliament re-assembled on the 20th of January, 1785. The Duke of Rutland was able to speak of the disturbances as past, and, in conjunction with the Premier, to seriously apply himself to the settlement of the difficulty. Influence, in the meantime, had been at work to induce the Volunteer forces to abstain from further interference in political or social questions; considerable success had attended the efforts so made, and many resigned their commissions. In his opening speech the Lord Lieutenant "lamented the lawless outrages and unconstitutional proceedings which had taken place since the prorogation, and expressed his satisfaction that they were confined to a few places, and even there condemned. He observed with pleasure that, by the salutary interposition of the laws, the general tranquillity was re-established. He directed attention in the King's name, to the consideration of those objects of trade and commerce between Great Britain and Ireland, which had not yet received their complete adjustment." The usual recommendations then followed. Mr. Flood took exception to the passage which stated the existence of "lawless outrage and unconstitutional proceeding," and moved an amendment directed towards Reform, which was negatived without a division. The usual address was voted. His Majesty in his answer thereto spoke in determined language of "the attempt to overawe Parliament." "His Majesty has observed with great concern, the popular disturbances that have lately prevailed from the intemperance and indiscretion of misguided men, and confides in the constant and strenuous endeavours of his faithful Commons of Ireland to prevent their pernicious effects, and their resolution to reject and suppress every assumed authority which may attempt to dictate to the legislature, affords his Majesty the highest satisfaction." A change had indeed taken place, when such words could be addressed to a Parliament which, three years previously, had accomplished its own independence by closely similar means. Mr. Grattan defended the Volunteers against the charge of complicity in the disturbances complained of; he drew the attention of the House to "the alarming measure of drilling the lowest classes of the populace, by which a stain had been brought on the character of the Volunteers;" he stigmatized the attempted Congress, and declared "that two sets of representatives, one *de jure*, and another supposing itself a representative *de facto*, cannot well exist." The House desired to conciliate the Volunteers, and to make amends for the aspersions which had been cast upon them; and resolved "That the Volunteers of Ireland have been eminently useful to their country, by the protection they afforded against a foreign enemy, by their present exertions in support of the police; and that this House highly approves of the conduct of those who, since the conclusion of the war, retired to cultivate the blessings of peace."

In answer to the invitation in the speech from the Throne, Mr. Orde brought forward his famous resolutions regarding the trade between Ireland and Great Britain. They were eleven in number. They had been altered and settled by the advice and with the assistance of Henry Grattan, and were considered by him "to be perfectly indispensable." He described them "as having a three-fold principle :—1. After the expenses of the nation are paid, to contribute to the general expenses of the Empire. 2. That by making the surplus not applicable to the general expense till all expenses are paid, it interests both the British and Irish Ministers in Irish economy. 3. To subject the surplus to the control of the Irish Parliament." He described the plan " as open, fair and just, and such as the British Minister can justify to both nations." The resolutions, after discussion, passed without much opposition. They were based on the principle of equalisation of duties in both countries. They preserved existing protections,—Ireland retained the privilege of fixing her own duties on her own productions, and could control the duties imposed on such articles in England. The result must have been to send a large English commerce to Ireland. They presented, however, opportunity for discord. The last resolution provided that " for the protection of trade, whenever the gross hereditary revenue of Ireland should exceed £650,000, the excess should be applied to the support of the Imperial fleet." Here lay the snare! Was Ireland to be a tributary nation to Great Britain? It was admitted that it was England's fleet, England's counsels, and England's influence, rendered such trade not only possible but safe. These advantages were considered as affording no justification in calling on Ireland to thus contribute. The resolution was modified to meet the views of the opponents, accepted by the Parliament, and transmitted to England. Pitt at once gave evidence of his friendly disposition to Ireland, of which he had previously exhibited many indications. He introduced the resolutions, and recommended the English Parliament to accept them. In order to put the two countries on a fair footing, he proposed to reduce the concessions to two heads :—1. The importation of the produce of our Colonies in the West Indies and America through Ireland into Great Britain. 2. A mutual exchange between the two countries of their respective productions and manufactures upon equal terms."* The linen trade of Ireland was to be continued as her monopoly. English manufacturing and commercial towns became alarmed;

* Plowden, vol. ii.

sixty-four petitions were presented against the resolution, that from Lancashire having 80,000 signatures. The alteration in the eleventh article gave colour, if not force, to their remonstrance and dissatisfaction. It was impossible, in the midst of the public agitation, to attempt to pass the Irish resolutions in the form in which they had been received. Pitt took them under his special care. He had them re-arranged with the view of what was just and equitable between the two countries. The period for the final adjustment of jealousies and differences had at length arrived. Both Parliaments were on their trial, and time was allowed for deliberation.

The Militia Act had expired. The necessity for the re-constitution of an armed force, under the direct control of the Crown, was obvious. The conduct of the Volunteers had alienated many supporters. They had, in defiance of the law, ranged themselves by the side of armed citizens for the purpose of insurrection. They were now objects of fear rather than of admiration. Opportunity offered to invite the well affected in their ranks to be enrolled in the service of the Crown, for which their volunteer exercises both fitted and pre-disposed them. On he 14th of February, Mr. Luke Gardiner moved "That the sum of £20,000 be granted to His Majesty for the purpose of clothing the Militia of this Kingdom." The discussion which followed afforded opportunity for contrasting the Volunteers as the champions of constitutional rights, and as the abettors of civil disturbances. In the former position they had won the gratitude of their country, and had given stability to her Councils; in the latter they had assisted in the defiance of law and subversion of social order, causing loss of life and great injury to property. The Attorney-General expressed himself in severe terms respecting them. "They had," he said, "admitted into their ranks a low description of men, and proceeded in a most unconstitutional manner." Mr. Grattan declared "the Volunteers had no right to be displeased at the establishment of a Militia, and if they had expressed displeasure the dictates of armed men ought to be disregarded by Parliament." He drew distinctions between the primitive Volunteers and the then existing force, and observed, "There is a cankered part of the dregs of the people that has been armed: let no gentleman give such men countenance, or pretend to join them with the original Volunteers." Mr. Gardiner's resolution was carried by 139—63.

The Parliament found time to pass a measure which has since been often quoted,* which provided "that holders of leases under charter school property, by applying within the first seven years of their lease, or of last renewal, and paying down one year's rent, with the cost of new leases, should of right be entitled to renewal for forty-one years; but no relief in law or equity if seven years elapse." This Act so far afforded security of tenure, and is the first statute that gives legal effect to what has since been known as "tenant right." [App. 14.]

The petitions against the Irish commercial resolutions led to certain modifications in a measure intended to be mutually binding. In the many changes of British mercantile obligations with those countries with whom Ireland was privileged to trade, not only under the resolutions, but by the laws then in force, it was anticipated that circumstances might arise when Great Britain might require to modify or abandon the existing obligations. It was necessary to provide against such a contingency, and accordingly the 4th of the English resolutions proposed:—

"That it is highly important to the general interests of the British Empire that the laws for regulating trade and navigation should be the same in Great Britain and Ireland, and, therefore, that it is essential towards carrying into effect the present settlement, that all laws which have been made, or shall be made, in Great Britain for securing exclusive privileges to the ships and mariners of Great Britain, Ireland, and the British Colonies and Plantations, and for regulating and restraining the trade of the British Colonies and Plantations, such laws imposing the same restraints and conferring the same benefits on the subjects of both Kingdoms, should be in force in Ireland by laws to be passed by the Parliament of that Kingdom for the same time and

* 25 Geo. III. c. 55.

in the same manner as in Great Britain." The ordinary reader might interpret this to mean on the part of England :—We freely extend to Ireland the full enjoyment of all our trade to these localities, subject to existing laws and restraints. Our benefits being equal, it is a condition, that should we, on whom the burden rests of our mutual and conjoint protection, find it necessary, in the interests of both, to vary those laws or restraints that you, Ireland, will co-operate with us, and adopt such changes in order that our reciprocal benefits may still continue to be the same. Ireland thought otherwise. She did not dissent from the modifications in the propositions, [for these were matters for compromise or arrangement. But—to be called on to re-enact English laws! Never! Grattan declared such a proposal to be "a revocation of the Constitution." The country was up in arms: all other English injustice was as nothing to this. Merchants and manufacturers raised an outcry which found an echo from the disaffected populace—we have asked for bread, you have given us a stone! The treachery of England was too manifest. Petitions poured in from all quarters against the proposed change. [App. 15.] Flood out-Grattaned Grattan; he described the resolutions "as an infamous attack on Irish Independence." "Freedom of Constitution was necessary to freedom of trade," "Liberty is the nurse of Commerce" were the commonplace expressions of the time. Appeals were made to the passions rather than to the judgments of those who found in the new opening for agitation a fresh opportunity for political display. It was to no purpose that Orde protested that England had no such designs as were imputed to her. The debate lasted all night, and, on the morning of the 13th of August, at nine o'clock, the utmost the Government could command for leave to bring in the Bill was 127—108.

When the result of the division was known, popular indignation rose to fever heat. Flood was for revolution rather than submit. An interval of two days was spent in meetings, remonstrances and revilings. On the 15th, when the Bill came on for discussion, Flood moved, "we hold ourselves bound not to enter into any engagement to give up the sole and exclusive right of Parliament to legislate for Ireland in all cases, externally, commercially, internally." It was in vain the Attorney-General declared that the Bill was in no way opposed to the free constitution of Ireland, or that the House was reminded it was asked to do no more than that which was its annual practice in every session since the Colonial trade was granted,—in reciting the British Act, and re-enacting it. To no purpose did he declare that every advantage which British subjects possessed was offered equally to Ireland, or that the House was reminded that without English protection their means of trading would be worthless. He spoke to the Irish Commons and Irish people in language of which, it is to be regretted, they had small experience — words of sober remonstrance and truth. His observations led to personal retort and individual insult, according to existing practices, to be settled outside the House. The division evidenced a diminished majority in comparison with that which had permitted the introduction of the Bill, and Mr. Orde announced the measure would be withdrawn.

Thus was another occasion, critical in the history of the country, permitted to pass. The public ecstasy, that is the satisfaction of political agitators, knew no bounds. The Constitution was saved. England's propositions were rejected, and Ireland's opportunity was lost.

In the debates on the Commercial question, Mr. D. Brown's observations, when Mr. Orde moved the adjournment of the House, ought to be quoted: "He seemed to think the arrangement impracticable. This arrangement, Sir, has suggested in the other country an idea, that I am almost afraid to mention to this House: —A Union! Good God! Sir, what union could we have with Great Britain, but union of debt and taxation—a union depriving us of liberty, and ruinous to our country?"

Parliament re-assembled on the 19th of January, 1786. Mr. Conolly, on the 9th of February, brought forward his motion for a general review of taxation. The House was in no mood to enter on the question, and it was lost by 134—78. A sense of disappointment was experienced in the House. It had won a victory, but how much had it lost? Many asked the question.

Why a measure against which so much feeling was expressed was capable of being carried, was also a subject of inquiry. Mr. Forbes believed the answer was to be found in the presence in Parliament of Members holding places and pensions. On the 6th of March he brought forward a motion respecting the pension list, which he declared exceeded that of Great Britain by several thousands, and amounted to £96,000 a year. On the 13th, he presented a Bill to limit their amount, and stated that in the two previous years pensions had increased by £16,000. Members who were above necessity, others above corruption, and some who had no hopes of purchase, supported his Bill. The Attorney-General opposed it on the grounds of prerogative, which, it is to be presumed, in his view, included a capacity for the purchase of votes. The pension list was declared to be a grievance; the pensioners however, voted for its continuance, and after a discussion, in which Mr. Grattan declared, "If he should vote that pensions were not a grievance, he should vote an impudent, an insolent, and a public lie;" the Bill was thrown out on its second reading by 134—78. The arguments of " Prerogative" in its support, were at least audacious, recollecting that, by the 6th of Anne c. 7, § 25, any member of the English Parliament, not being an officer in the army or navy, accepting a new commission, who accepted any office of profit under the Crown, vacated his seat thereby, unless it be one created prior to 25th October, 1705 ; and by 22 Geo. III., c. 45, disqualification attended those holding contracts with the Crown. There is but one explanation of arguments, supported neither by law nor facts ;—the depraved state of public feeling which rendered the Government desirous of adopting a Machiavellian doctrine, and of retaining their capacity to do evil that good might come.

To duly estimate the action of Parliament on the next matter brought under their consideration, it is necessary to review the social condition of Dublin at this period. The City was practically under the rule of mob-law. Associations publicly sat, in defiance of all authority, to dictate to members and others their conduct in public matters. Were their dictates not attended to, destruction of property, or injury to the person, most certainly followed. A "tarring and feathering" committee inflicted punishment less permanent in its effects than that of the "Houghers:"—"Slashers," or armed ruffians, whose object it was to disfigure, exercised a terrorism over the quiet citizens, whose sole protection against such outrage were a few local constables, generally the companions or friends of the offenders. The recent riots had demonstrated the necessity of some force intermediate between the military and people, which might be under the control of the civil magistracy. With this object, the Attorney-General on the 17th of March, 1786, introduced a "Police Bill,"—"for the better execution of the law in the City of Dublin, and the parts adjacent." It proposed to supersede the authority of the Mayor and Aldermen of the city, and to appoint seven, afterwards reduced to three, paid magistrates, and forty constables, mounted or on foot as occasion required, and gave them authority to enter and search houses where there was reason to believe arms were concealed. This exceptional power was a necessity of the times. It was known that the liberties of the city had many houses in which nightly meetings of the most treasonable character were held. That rebellion and disaffection were openly preached, and that weapons of various kinds were being collected to arm the populace, to whose aid, against the English Government, foreign assistance was even then being negotiated for. In supporting the Bill, the Attorney-General stated "that the Catholic rabble had become possessed of the arms of the Volunteers, that when the mob outraged the House of Commons, the Mayor, though warned of the approaching riot, was powerless to prevent it." Under such circumstances, it might have been expected men of independence would have considered true liberty to consist in freedom of action, undismayed by fears of subsequent injury:—the Irish patriots thought otherwise. Grattan offered uncompromising opposition to the measure, and declared, "that under pretence of preserving the peace of the city, it was an attempt to destroy its Independence." His arguments were addressed to the prejudices and passions of the people, through the medium of the senate. He moved that the Bill be committed that day three months. His motion was lost by 139—37. So many places were to be filled, and the offices were consistent with a seat in the House; as many incorruptible patriots were anxious to serve the Crown, the places were not disposed of, and the efforts of the Government deserved their support. Baffled in his opposition, Mr. Grattan moved "that the Commissioners should not sit in Parliament." The aphorism of Flood prevailed, that "a patriot in office was more useful to his country," and the motion was lost by a large majority, including the votes of so many desirous to serve her in the new police. Mr. Grattan next attempted to limit the power of the Lord Lieutenant in the appointments; in this also he was defeated. The Bill was carried in spite of his opposition, and additional instruments were thereby afforded for strengthening the hands of the Government.*

There is no doubt this last division was a trial of strength, and satisfied the Opposition that defeat awaited any further effort to embarrass.

It was intended by the Government that, should the Police Bill prove a success in the Metropolis, its provisions would be further extended. The opposition it had received was not encouraging. In the meantime necessity for action was urgent to repress outrages throughout the country. The social condition of the Irish peasant has been already mentioned. His abject poverty had nothing to redeem it. His landlord, if resident, was so embarrassed that he could afford neither encouragement nor assistance. If absent, his agent was but a machine to exact the uttermost farthing of rent as it became due. Added to this, the burden of tithes pressed heavily on the people. Many of the rectors were pluralists and non-residents. The major part of their revenues was derived from those professing the Roman Catholic faith. Is it to be wondered at that an organised resistance prevailed to prevent the levy of tithes, which came with the double stigma of being a premium for clerical extortion, as well as a tribute to an alien faith? A Bill was introduced for the better protection of the clergy in the south. In the course of its discussion it became evident that the exaction of tithes was so oppressive that Government thought it right to abandon any special or exclusive measure, and to postpone till the next sitting the consideration of what means were most advisable for the general protection of all residents against the attacks of those local banditti, who, under various names, exercised terrorism in defiance of law. The postponement gave new strength to White-Boyism. Riot and disorder held high revel, notwithstanding all efforts for their repression. This necessitated the introduction of repressive measures. Recourse to Parliament was the safest means at the disposal of the Viceroy. Biennial Sessions often rendered delays most dangerous. The Viceroy determined to break through the rule, and to summon Parliament at the beginning of the year 1787. The House accordingly assembled on the 13th February. The Attorney-General introduced a Bill to prevent " tumultuous risings," which led to an animated discussion. As originally proposed it gave power to pull down any Roman Catholic chapel in which meetings of disaffected people might be held, and to prevent any chapel so pulled down from being rebuilt for three years. This clause was abandoned, and the Bill became law from the 25th day of March, 1787,* by which, if persons to the number of twelve met in an unlawful and riotous manner, and did not disperse within one hour, when required by a Justice of the Peace so to do, their offence was felony punishable by death. Pulling down religious houses, or obstructing clergy, was a like offence. Administering an unlawful oath received transportation for life, with other penalties proportionately severe for minor crimes. Mr. Grattan recognised the fact that to legislate for grievances, and leave the cause of the grievances unredressed, was to give legal support to oppression. On the 13th day of March, he brought forward a motion as a precursor to an intended Bill, " that if at the commencement of the next Session of Parliament it shall appear that public tranquility has been restored in those parts of the Kingdom that have been lately disturbed, and due obedience be paid to the laws, this House will take into consideration the

* 27 Geo. III. c. 15.

subject of tithes, and endeavour to form some plan for the honourable support of the clergy and the ease of the people." The motion was strongly opposed by the Government, who argued that the time was improper; that passing such a resolution would be to capitulate with insurrection, and to offer a reward for that obedience to the laws on which they had a right to insist. Yielding to the arguments advanced, the resolution was not pressed to a division.

The effects of the Attorney-General's Act were what might have been anticipated. Assemblies in force were discontinued, and comparative quiet restored. The Duke of Rutland determined to try what had never previously failed—the Vice-Regal presence. He visited Munster, the most disaffected of all the counties, and was, in all directions, well received. Comparative quiet followed and with its restoration trade revived. Both countries seemed weary of contention. Their commercial relations passively settled down into mutual concessions, no vexatious questions being raised on either side; so much so, that there was an opportunity for directing the attention of the Legislature to other wants than those satisfied by repressive Acts.

The Navigation Act was declared to be in force in Ireland in a Bill* for Improving the Navigation, which led to an amendment on the part of Mr. Grattan, the purport of which was "that the Navigation Act, 12 Ch. 2, should bind His Majesty's subjects of Ireland, so long as it shall have the effect of conferring the same benefits, and imposing the same restrictions on both Kingdoms." This was lost by 127—52. Its terms contrast strangely with the provision in the fourth commercial resolution, and seem to be identical in principle; and yet, to this latter, Mr. Grattan offered most uncompromising opposition, which was the chief means of preventing "the final adjustment."

It may be a relief, for a time, to turn from the grave cares of State, and consider the great Sedan question, if only as an illustration of the tone of the petitions, and the preponderance of sentiment entering into Irish grievances. Sedan chairs, when

* 27 Geo. III. c. 23.

privately licensed, paid duty of £1 15s 6d a year, which formed part of the funds of the Lying-in Hospital. Public chairs were under the control of the police. An order was made by the Police Commissioners "That no person should ply or carry any Hackney Sedan Chair defective in any part or particular ; that they should be carried by able men, decent in apparel and of good and civil behaviour ; that they should not be carried on the flagged way ; that the chairmen should have numbered badges on their breasts, and, in addition to the number on the chair, the number and name of the proprietor stamped or painted on the inner side of the poles."* This was made the subject of a petition, and seriously occupied the attention of a Committee of Parliament. The Chairmen alleged "the order was a grievance ; that theirs was a peculiar trade, that defects might exist without their knowledge, that the owners of chairs employed by nobility and gentry could not be answerable for men acting in their absence ; that 'able men' were vague terms, and 'decent apparel' a question rather of means than the opinion of the wearer ; that not to carry a chair on the flagged way was 'an encroachment on the rights of humanity;' that to wear a badge on the breast was an act of wanton oppression, and the having the names inside the poles altogether unnecessary." A select Committee was for days occupied on these weighty questions, and reported on the 11th March, 1778,† " 1st. That the Petitioners have fully proved the allegations of their Petition ; 2nd. That in the opinion of this Committee three numbers on each side, and another on back are sufficient to identify owners of the chair, the numbers and the owners being registered with the Commissioners of Police. 3rd. That it is the opinion of the Committee that the chairmen of the City of Dublin are an honest, laborious, and decent body of men, and highly deserving the protection and relief of Parliament." The said Report was ordered to lie on table for perusal of Members. It must have been gratifying to the chairmen of Dublin to know that the interests and rights of their brother professionals occupied almost the last clause in the last act of the Irish Parliament. [App. 16.]‡

---

* Com. Jour. 24 Dec. 1787.   † Com. Jour., 11 March, 1778.
‡ 10 Geo. III, c. 100, §. 63.

The close of the Session of 1787 brought with it much personal sorrow to the Irish people in the death of their Viceroy. The Duke of Rutland was attacked by the Irish scourge—Typhus fever, and after a few days' illness expired, to the generally expressed regrets of all classes. A word in his behalf may be permitted. Profuse in his expenditure, agreeable in his bearing, strong in his resolves, and confident in his advisers, the Duke of Rutland won the kind feeling, and commanded the confidence of the Irish people. He was popular with the crowd; he knew their weaknesses, —appreciated, and when he could do so, gratified them. He understood the temper of the Irish House of Commons, and on impending divisions neglected no means to conciliate opponents and to further secure friends. During a period requiring tact, discretion, and boldness, with promptitude in action, he proved equal to the occasion ; and under circumstances of great pressure, in dealing with venal senators, he neither heavily encumbered the exchequer, nor unduly strained the prerogative of the Crown. A less-gifted diplomatist, in stemming popular disturbance, might have incited to open rebellion, or, in controlling the House of Commons, have invited to revolution. He skilfully avoided either extreme ; and it is something to his credit that his highest eulogy came from many to whom he was politically opposed. He died in office, and may be fairly said to have accomplished the duty he had specially undertaken.

It was no easy matter to select a suitable successor to a Viceroy who, in times of difficulty and peril, had guided the State through dangers impossible to be too gravely estimated. The appointment of Earl Temple was considered appropriate. The Irish had already had experience of his administration. He had, since leaving Ireland, progressed in the Peerage, and it was hoped that as Marquis of Buckingham, with large Irish estates, he would bring the landed gentry of the country to his side. The active steps taken for the vindication of the law having restored comparative quiet, it was anticipated that time and opportunity would be found for the redress of those social grievances complained of. The arrival of their old acquaintance was to the inhabitants of Dublin an occasion for the display of popular enthusiasm ; the horses were taken from his carriage, and the people, with every demonstration of satisfaction, drew it through the streets. It would not have been very difficult to have maintained the popularity then aroused, but the Marquis of Buckingham entirely failed to do so. The Irish admire firmness; they respect, even when they fear, the exercise of a resolute will; they love liberality, and glory in extravagance; but,—they despise sham! The Duke of Rutland in the former respects had satisfied their ideas of a Viceroy. So long as the ends of public justice were accomplished, he did not too curiously investigate the means. The additional burden of £20,000 a-year imposed on the revenue of the country during his administration may have been the cheapest and best compromise under the circumstances. The expenditure on the Court was lavish; there had been no desire to discourage similar outlay elsewhere. The Marquis of Buckingham was of a very different disposition. The Castle festivities were diminished, the household expenses curtailed, the official accounts scrutinized. It is but fair to say that many of the inquiries instituted were forced on the Viceroy, and did not result from any captious spirit. When formerly in office certain ordnance returns had been submitted to him; it had been his duty to examine them, and when, on his re-arrival, reports from the same department were again submitted, the glaring differences left no alternative but their investigation and an exposure of the frauds practised. The heads and clerks in many public departments took the alarm; many resigned and were permitted to pass unpunished; by those less implicated a cry was raised, that meanness under the name of thrift was but a pretext to induce officials to retire, that personal friends or dependants might fill their places. This insinuation received apparent support from certain alterations in the Board of Revenue, whereby the Commissioners were increased in number, and Englishmen introduced. Official corruption was on its trial! The friends of Reform believed the Augean stable would be cleared, and the public expenses proportionately diminished; and so they might have been, had not evil fortune in the shape of temptation ordered otherwise. One of the most valuable sinecures in Ireland, the office of Chief Remembrancer, became vacant. The pay was

£4,000 a-year, with patronage. The Marquis had a brother, whom he nominated to the post, and thereby all expectants were equally aggrieved. Honest men denounced the job, while knaves exclaimed of the Viceroy, "he is one of us"! After such an illustration of official reform, it became, on the part of those assailed, a mere struggle for time. No nation detects imposture sooner than the Irish. Those whose positions were in jeopardy were convinced the opportunity was not far distant when they might retaliate. In these views, however, they underrated the intelligence and vigour of the Viceroy; the opportunity arrived, but not in the manner they had anticipated. His popularity was not only short lived, but with the public disappointment came a revulsion of feeling, which eventuated in his positive detestation.

Parliament was chiefly occupied in the repression of local disturbances. Mr. Grattan believed the opportunity was favourable for again bringing forward the question of Tithes. On the 14th February he moved for a Committee, and in an exhaustive speech reviewed the wrongs thereby occasioned; his arguments were admitted, but his remedies denied by 121—49. A Bill was introduced by the Secretary of State "to enable all ecclesiastical persons and bodies in certain counties to recover a just compensation for the tithes withheld from them in the year 1787, against such persons as were liable to the same." The Bill proposed to dispense with trial by jury, and to determine by assessment before a judge what sums should be paid. This, after active opposition, passed into Law.

The Session of 1789 was opened by the announcement of the serious illness of the King. The Commons voted an Address suitable to the occasion. It, however, contained an allusion to the Viceroy, which afforded Mr. Grattan an opportunity of reviewing his conduct in office. He pointed out that the Marquis's desire for retrenchment was but affectation, and declared that "he was not only a jobber, but a jobber in a mask;" further affirming that "his administration had not only been expensive," but "that his expenses were accompanied by hypocrisy." Mr. Brown, of the College, (as the Member for the University of Dublin is termed in the Reports), characterized his economy "as a little gnawing, corroding, venomous scrutiny, which eats its way into the hearts of poor men, who had not strength of body to bear violent accusations, or strength of mind enough to retort on great offenders ; which seemed to look out for crimes and forfeitures as objects of prey, not of correction."* The circumstance of the illness of the King prevented a hostile division.

On February 11th, 1789, the House of Commons took into their consideration the subject of His Majesty's illness. The Attorney-General said it would be necessary that the proceedings in Ireland should be carried on in the same manner as in England. Mr. Grattan contended that it was not so, and repudiated any servile imitation of the proceedings of another country, "not in the choice of a Regent, for that is a common concern, but in the particular provisions and limitations which ought to be, and must be, governed by the particular circumstances of the different countries." After a long and learned speech he concluded by a resolution, "that it is the opinion of this Committee that the personal exercise of the Royal authority is, by His Majesty's indisposition, for the present interrupted." Mr. Conolly further moved an Address to the Prince of Wales, requesting him, "under the style and title of Prince Regent of Ireland, in the name of His Majesty, to exercise and administer, according to the Laws and Constitution of the Kingdom, all regal powers, jurisdictions, and prerogatives to the Crown and Government thereof belonging." The Attorney-General referred to the Act of the fourth of William and Mary, cap. 1, sec. 1, the Act of Recognition, which set forth the Union of the Kingdom of Ireland to the Crown of England. He argued that the executive being the same, the Regent should be the same. He pointed out that the Act of 1782 had rendered the Great Seal of England necessary to the passing of any Irish Law. He read the amendment to that Act, proposed by Mr. Flood, as proof of the authority the King exercised ; and declared that if the Prince did not accept the Regency, and the Address should reach him, it would call on him to act in defiance of the statute which makes

* Plow., vol. ii. 231.

the Crown inseparable. The motion was, notwithstanding, carried without a division. On the 17th, the Lord Lieutenant laid before the Irish Parliament the resolutions agreed to in the English House. They were identical in spirit with those of the Irish, except that they limited the power of the Regent in granting peerages, creating offices, or charging any part of His Majesty's real or personal estate. They also provided for the care of the King. The reply of His Royal Highness, accepting the duties of the position as offered, accompanied the resolutions. These, however, had no effect on the Irish Parliament, and they persisted in the terms of their original Address. They did so, though assured by the Attorney-General he considered it as tending to dethrone the King. On the 18th it was agreed that both Houses should carry to the Lord Lieutenant the Address as determined on. The Lords and Commons, with the Chancellor and Speaker at their head, went in procession to the Castle, and the Address was delivered. When the House of Commons assembled, the Speaker informed them that he had attended the Lord Lieutenant, and that his Excellency had returned the following answer: "Under the impressions which I feel of my official duty, and of the oaths which I have taken as Chief Governor of Ireland, I am obliged to decline transmitting this Address to Great Britain; for I cannot consider myself warranted to lay before the Prince of Wales an Address purporting to invest His Royal Highness with power to take upon him the Government of this realm before he shall be enabled by law to do so." In this resolve the English Cabinet "entirely concurred." The House on this information adjourned. At its next meeting Mr. Grattan moved that a competent number of members be appointed by the House to present the Address to His Royal Highness. In his observations on the answer of the Lord Lieutenant, he concluded by a motion, "that the Lords and Commons of Ireland have exercised an undoubted right and discharged an indispensable duty, to which in the present emergency they alone are competent." The Attorney-General again argued, "that both countries were committed by the measure; that the principles of the Address were pernicious and unconstitutional; that the claim set up by the two

Houses of Parliament was illegal and unfounded; that the connexion between the two countries was shaken by it, and the security by which men held their property in Ireland was endangered; that the Lords and Commons of Ireland had not a shadow of right to provide by their authority for the executive Government of Ireland, and that if the Lord Lieutenant had transmitted the Address, he would have subjected himself to impeachment." Discussion on minor points was raised, and in the end Mr. Grattan's motion was carried by 115—83. Thus triumphant, the House determined to retaliate. Mr. Grattan moved "That His Excellency the Lord Lieutenant's answer to both Houses of Parliament is ill-advised, contains an unwarranted and unconstitutional censure on the proceedings of both Houses of Parliament, and attempts to question the undoubted rights and privileges of the Lords Spiritual and Temporal and the Commons of Ireland." It was in vain the Attorney-General protested. He had but the one course open, to move an amendment as an addition, and this he did as follows: "Although this House cannot know the impressions of official duty, nor the obligations of the oath under which His Excellency feels himself obliged to act, and although His Royal Highness the Prince of Wales is not as yet invested with the powers of Regent in Great Britain." The amendment was rejected by 119—78. Mr. Burgh then moved a further amendment to the original motion, to come in at its end, "of making a Regent of Ireland without law, and whom we know not to be Regent of Great Britain." This was lost by the same majority which carried the original motion.

The Government was thus defeated on a most important trial of strength:—the explanation of the defeat was yet to become apparent.

The Irish House of Lords appointed two of its members—the Duke of Leinster and the Earl of Charlemount—and the House of Commons appointed four members on their behalf, together to present the Address of both Houses to His Royal Highness the Prince of Wales.

The deputation proceeded to London, and presented the Address. The Prince, in his answer, expressed his gratitude, but delayed his final reply. He observed, "the fortunate change which has taken place in the circumstances which gave occasion to the Address induces me for a few days to delay giving a final answer, trusting that the joyful event of His Majesty's resuming the personal exercise of His Royal authority may then render it only necessary for me to repeat those sentiments of gratitude and affection for the loyal and generous people of Ireland, which I feel indelibly imprinted on my heart." On the 14th of March, it was announced from the Throne that His Majesty had recovered. On the 20th, the final answer of the Prince of Wales was received. It conveyed the usual compliments and assurances:—and it did more, as the first paragraph concluded, " Nothing can obliterate from my memory and my gratitude *the principles* upon which that arrangement was made, and the circumstances by which it was attended." It further added, " I shall not pay so ill a compliment to the Lords and Commons of Ireland as to suppose that they were mistaken in their reliance on the moderation of my views and the purity of my intentions. A manly confidence, directing the manner of proceeding towards those who entertain sentiments becoming the high situation to which they are born, furnishes the most powerful motive to the performance of their duty, at the same time that the liberality of sentiment, which, in conveying a trust confers an honour, can have no tendency to relax that provident vigilance and that public jealousy which ought to watch over the exercise of power." The answer proceeds—" personally I cannot but regret your departure. I have had an opportunity of acquiring a knowledge of your private characters, and it has added to the high esteem which I have before entertained for you on account of your public merits."

This pointed allusion to " the principles on which the arrangement was made," and to " the manly confidence " directing the manner of proceeding refers to the difference between the Address of the English and of the Irish Parliaments. The answer of the Regent was attributed to the pen of Charles Fox, and placed at rest for a time his ambitious expectations. There can be no doubt that the sudden and unexpected convalescence of the King was the occasion of the greatest political discomfiture which scheming senators and their political leaders ever encountered. It occurred thus : The previous summer had been spent by Mr. Grattan in England, where he had exchanged confidences with the Whig leaders, and had heard and shared in their bitter animosities against Pitt, who was firmly rooted in office, and enjoyed the confidence with the favour of the King. The Royal strength had been proved on all political emergencies. The King was an attentive observer of passing events. The distractions in France, and the many disquietudes at home, acting on the mind of His Majesty, already indicating predisposition to disorder, eventuated in unmistakeable delirium. A Regency sooner or later seemed inevitable. Fox was the companion and trusted friend of the Prince. Once the Regent was established, Ministers and measures would be changed. The question of Regency and the powers to be granted had been discussed. Pitt, knowing the predilections of the Prince, was for limited authority, Fox was in support of an unconditional appointment. The Prince, in pointed phrases, resented personally limitations* which he was powerless to resist officially. Grattan coincided with Fox's views, and determined on their adoption in Ireland, in the confident expectation of their refusal by the Marquis of Buckingham, and in such an event of his consequent removal from office. It was at the time politically known that Fox, in anticipation of his accession to office, promised Grattan that the Viceroy should be recalled, and Lord Spenser, known to be a friend to Roman Catholic relief, should take his place. Grattan saw himself thereby once again master of the situation. In this expectation he returned to Ireland, and soon aroused in the minds of his adherents that jealous spirit of nationality in which each desired an opportunity to excel. It was to no purpose the Attorney-General tried to recall them to reason. Those who were creatures of pay thought the opportunity safe to exercise an independence to which they had long been strangers. They cared not for the Constitution, but for themselves, and easily adopted views suggested by the coming men. Many who hoped that their turn might come,

* Plowden, vol. ii.

also took up the cry—Ireland was her own mistress ; she would choose her own Regent, and on her own terms. Mr. Grattan, not content with carrying his resolution and his vote of censure, moved, when Mr. Mason brought forward his Bill for the year's supply, an amendment changing the time to two months, which was carried by 102—77. His object was to force the Marquis of Buckingham to resign, and to prevent a prorogation or dissolution. The personal bitterness entertained towards the Viceroy is shown in the concluding observations of Mr. Grattan in reply to the Attorney-General : " As to the House having quarrelled with the Lord-Lieutenant, the right hon. gentleman has stated a wrong position ; it was not the House that quarrelled with the Lord-Lieutenant, but it was the Lord-Lieutenant that quarrelled with us, and it is wise to prevent him from carrying a measure of revenge into execution."* It was to no purpose the Attorney-General indignantly protested. He declared he was sorry to see the spirit of White-Boyism manifesting itself in Parliament. He alluded to a combination, in the form of a Round Robin, that was publicly known. [App. 17.]. It was Mr. Brownlow who had cautioned the House, that if supplies were granted for the usual time, a prorogation might ensue, as had been the case in the Townsend administration. The Attorney-General, in his retort, reminded the members " that the Parliament so treated had voted the Viceroy a vote of thanks," observing that " the majority which passed it had cost the nation half a million ;" and he added, in appreciation of those present, " if Mr. Grattan's motion was carried, it might lead to a similar address, which would cost half a million more, and he should therefore oppose it," concluding his speech by declaring that it was his intention to move "that it is the undoubted right of the Lords and Commons to exercise and enjoy every office of profit and trust within the realm."

All was ready for action, and all were expectant, when news arrived of the recovery of the King. Fifty-seven placemen, or dependants (twenty Peers, and thirty-seven Commoners), who

* Plowden. vol. ii.. p. 132.

were creatures of the Crown by the honourable title of purchase, were especially in dismay. The Marquis of Buckingham had before him a copy of the "Robin." One whom they more feared, the Attorney-General, had it in his power to retaliate ; and both let it be known that they waited but the opportunity.

Confident in his majorities, and not anticipating the announcement of the 1st of March, when official information of the King's health reached Dublin, Mr. Grattan had prepared his friends for his intended campaign against the Marquis of Buckingham. The appointment of his brother was to be set aside. The Pension Bill was to be carried, and the Police Bill repealed. It was too late to retreat—that would be to confess weakness ; to go forward was to court defeat. He was, however, compelled to take action, and for this reason : It was stated that to Grattan it was due that by the Bill of 1782 the Seal of Great Britain was necessary for Irish laws. Mr. Parsons, in the House, had commented on his "bungling," whilst the Dublin press adopted the phrase, and affirmed the liberality of the people had been too hastily bestowed. On the 3rd of March Mr. Grattan brought forward his resolutions respecting the grants of offices in reversion. He was, as usual, strong in his resentment against the Viceroy. The Attorney-General, who had received assurances of support from the wanderers, moved the adjournment, which was carried by a majority of nine. Mr. Forbes introduced his Place Bill, which provided for limiting pensions. The Government were apathetic on the matter, and it was carried so far as to limit pensions to £80,000 a year ; but it was thrown out in the House of Lords as " a measure designed to shut the door at a time when every exertion had to be made."* The further motions directed against Revenue officers having seats in Parliament, and against the Police Bill, were defeated by large majorities, so eager were the offenders to recover favour. Their betrayal had been flagrant : they were, notwithstanding their returning alligence, informed the penalties would be exacted. They appealed to the Attorney-General— their humiliation thereby must have been as abject as their

---

* P. C. Lord Buckingham to Lord Sydney.

submission was complete. The Marquis of Buckingham, in his letter to Lord Sydney, stated "he had not hesitated to authorize the Attorney-General to declare that it was not his intention to recommend to his Majesty the dismissal of the Gentlemen with whom he had conversed, or that of those who might accede immediately to the same declaration of submission. It is, however, expressly declared that the King's Government is under no engagement for future favour or countenance, either in their counties or elections, to any of those noblemen or gentlemen, and it is equally stipulated that any engagements to those who have zealously and uniformly supported Government shall be maintained, though the arrangement may interfere with the former engagements which had been made to those members when supporting the Administration." The Duke of Leinster and the Ponsonbies made no personal supplication. They clamoured for a "General Amnesty." They had been of the deputation, and they were dismissed—the Duke from the office of Master of the Rolls, which in the present day would be thought an extraordinary appointment, Ponsonby from the Board of Revenue, and others paid a similar penalty. Those who were spared became examples of political regeneration and loud in their praises of the Viceroy; congratulating themselves they were not as other men. This victory was not achieved without its price. Independent members were hard to be convinced. It cost £13,000 a year in the form of pensions, while to those of less material ambition rank was offered—nine Peers gaining a step, and seven members of the House of Commons being elevated to the Upper House. Well might the Lord Lieutenant be assured that "one hundred and ten servants of the Crown had been disciplined into obedience by the punishment of the mutineers."*

At this juncture (April, 1789) Lord Lifford resigned the Great Seal and Fitz-Gibbon became Lord Chancellor, being the first Irishman raised to that dignity. Deprived of the able and incorruptible aid of his Attorney-General in the House of Commons, Lord Buckingham declined to continue in office, and

* Froude, vol. 2. p. 519.

closed a Viceroyalty, which, but for his personal meanness and the inexcusable error of his brother's appointment, might have been regarded as not entirely failing to give effect to the policy of his predecessor.

That the presence of Fitz-Gibbon in the House of Commons was a tower of strength is evidenced in every debate where the interests of his country or the prerogative of the Crown were under consideration. An able lawyer, an accomplished orator, an experienced debater, an incorruptible senator, with, in his own person, a Spartan sense of public virtue, and undisguised contempt for State hirelings calling themselves patriots, he boldly faced each difficulty as it arose, and did not hesitate to publicly avow his opinions, holding the discharge of his duty as above all popular comment. To his unflinching personal courage was due the suppression of the most serious disturbance the country had been threatened with; and to his well known firmness may be ascribed the passive obedience to the law, which, in the attachment of the Sheriff, he had announced his determination to enforce. That one designed by nature to guide men by his genius should often have been compelled to listen to the sordid bargaining of those to whom the interest of their country was confided, is not the least strange illustration of these strange times. The best that can be said in his justification, if justification it be, is that what he did he did effectively and well, for the good, as he believed, of his country. Men knew and feared him. He appreciated and despised them. Knowing him so well, political bargains were, in State emergencies, with the exception of the Robin, faithfully carried out. When on the Regency question, the trustees of their country proved not only corrupt, but also mendacious, those who feared they might be "Victims of their Votes" found, in his public reproof and personal contempt, their severest punishment.

The opening of the Session of January, 1790, by the new Viceroy, the Earl of Westmoreland, was as the quiet after a storm. His speech contained but the every-day topics, as "the secure enjoyment of the blessings of peace, and the inestimable advantages arising from our free Constitution." Grattan and his party had experienced all the bitterness and exasperation of an ignominious defeat; and, what was worse than disappointment, they had disclosed their intentions to the English Minister, and placed him on his guard against their future movements. Mr. Grattan, in his speech on the Address, reviewed the past Session, and declared " the conduct of Ministers was little less than a daring outrage on the liberties and morals of the people, for at no period had so many instances of corruption and coercion occurred." He complained " that the Civil List had in five years increased to £30,000 a year, and the Military List to £100,000." He described the police " as an unconstitutional and corrupt influence in the Corporation of the City," and " a place army to encourage accomplices against the country." His personal vituperation of the late Viceroy was directed through the House to the people, who, with some knowledge of recent events, were curious to observe his conduct under his new reverse.

On February the 1st Mr. Grattan moved an address regarding the appointment of certain Commissioners, which enabled him to review in detail the late Government abuses he complained of. His speech at least informed the country of what he believed to be the conduct of the executive, supported by majorities in Parliament : " No Constitutional Bills to heal, no popular Bills to pacify. The Currency—the pure poison unmixed, unquenched, unqualified, or, if qualified, tempered only with revenge. On this principle did the Ministers take into their venal and vindictive hand the table of proscriptions ; on this principle, did they remove, not because the place was unnecessary—they had made unnecessary offices ; on this principle, did they deprive, not because the pension list was overburdened—they had augmented that list ; but because the placemen so removed and the pensioners so deprived had voted against the will of the Minister in questions wherein that Minister was pronounced to be unconstitutional, and known to be corrupt ;" and pressing his observations specially towards recent abuses, he added : " Sir, you have in Ireland no axe, and therefore no good minister." Mr. Conolly and others, who had subscribed " the Robin," followed in a similar strain. Mr. Parsons contended that the system, if persisted in, would deprive the country of all the acquisitions of 1782. The motion was lost by 160—50.

In no wise disconcerted by Mr. Grattan's failure on a similar motion, Mr. Forbes brought forward an address on the expenses of the nation, a subject which invited to free expressions of opinion. Mr. Grattan declared—"Was Ireland as much cast off by Providence as by her Ministers I own I should think her a country too lost to be defended." The division was as usual: 153—65. The conduct of the Marquis of Buckingham was next reviewed in a motion for a select Committee to inquire into the corrupt agreements for the sale of Peerages, and the purchase of seats in the House of Commons. The learning on the subject was exhausted, but the whole pith of the argument rested in the following reflections on Fitz-Gibbon's remarks, the sting of discomfiture still smarting : "If the nature of the measures did not import their own criminality and mischief, yet the conversation of the projectors had been full and explanatory on the subject : any money for a majority, give us the Treasury and we buy the Parliament ! but conversations of this sort have even entered these walls—these new charges are political expedients. Ireland was sold for £1,500,000 formerly, and if opposition persists will be sold again." Mr. Grattan concluded, "We charge them with committing these offences not in one, nor in two, but in many instances ; for which complication of offences we say they are impeachable ; guilty of a systematic endeavour to undermine the Constitution in violation of the laws of the land. We pledge ourselves to convict them, we dare them to go into an inquiry ; we do not affect to treat them as other than public malefactors ; we speak to them in a style of the most mortifying and humiliating defiance. We pronounce them to be public criminals ; will they dare to deny the charge ? I call upon, and dare the ostensible member to rise in his place, and say, on his honour, that he does not believe such corrupt agreements have taken place. I wait for a specific answer." Major Hobart replied : "I rise to say that if I could think the right honourable gentleman had any right to ask me the question he has proposed, and I were alone concerned in it, I should find no manner of difficulty in answering him ; but it is a question which relates to the exercise of His Majesty's undoubted prerogative; it would ill become me, upon the instigation of an individual, to say what were the reasons which induced His Majesty to bestow upon any persons those honours which the Crown alone can constitutionally confer." Motion lost by 172—60. Imagine such a charge, from one so eminent, being at the present day preferred against the Ministry in the English Commons, and so avowed being so answered! Mr. Forbes brought forward his Place and his Pensions' Bills, which met with their usual fate. On March 26th he introduced his Responsibility Bill for "securing a responsibility in the servants of the Crown in the different departments of the executive Government in Ireland, to the Parliament thereof." This Bill required the acts of the executive power to be signed by certain officers resident in Ireland, who, as Grattan stated, "should, with their lives and fortunes, be responsible to this Kingdom in the measures and expenses of Government." It was lost by 131—64. One motion, to the credit of the Session be it recorded, was carried—that of Mr. David Latouche : " That it is the opinion of this House, that the excessive use of spirituous liquors is highly injurious to the health and morals of the people ; that a Committee be appointed to take the subject into their consideration." The Session was further occupied by renewed attacks on the Police Bill, and the Peerage question, revived by Mr. Curran, in which he declared that " a contract had been entered into by the Ministers to raise to the Peerage certain persons on condition of their purchasing a certain number of seats in this House. It was a corrupt disposal of public money, it was an attempt to undermine the liberties of the people, and constituted a crime that deserved punishment. He pledged himself to prove the charge, if the House would agree to go into the inquiry." Mr. Ponsonby declared " that he had proof that Peerages had been sold for money," and added, " Go into a Committee, and if I do not establish my charge, degrade me—let me no longer enjoy the character of an honest man. I dare the administration to it. I risk my reputation on establishing the fact." The motion was lost.

Thus perpetually assailed, always on the defensive, the Government welcomed, in April, the natural dissolution of a Parliament which, under the form of Constitutional proceedings, had thrown away the opportunity for the regeneration of the country.

Lord Temple had inaugurated this Parliament by instituting the new Order of the Knights of St. Patrick, March 1783, which placed at the disposal of the Ministers honours to bestow. The Whig Club was formed at its termination, wherein discomfited politicians might find free expressions for their opinions, without the restrictions of Parliamentary utterance, which at no time seem to have been severe. The common ground of Country, her wrongs and their remedy, were their alleged bond of union. The blue and buff uniform survives to this our day, and is occasionally to be met with in gentlemen of the old school, who speak of the politics of their fathers, and are unwilling to confess how closely their then Whiggery approached the theories of political doctrinaires, and how nearly it proved subversive of the Throne.

The election of 1790 contrasts strangely with that which preceded it. The Parliament of 1782 represented an armed yet loyal people, true in their allegiance to the Crown, and explicit in the avowal of their grievances. They had firmly yet fairly demanded from England the restoration of their constitutional rights and privileges, and they had been met in a spirit of concession which satisfied their requirements. The law then passed in their behalf was declared to be "a measure of consummate wisdom and justice, suitable to the dignity and eminence of both nations, exalting the character of both, and furnishing a perpetual pledge of mutual amity." The concession granted had been "unaccompanied by any stipulation or condition whatever, the good faith and generosity with the honour of the nation, being regarded as the best guarantees that they would promote and perpetuate the harmony, stability and the glory of the Empire." The Parliament of 1783 entered on the discharge of their duties to the country in order to give effect to these anticipations. The time and circumstances were peculiarly favourable to give spirit to commercial pursuits. "Both Kingdoms," to further quote the address of Lord Northington, "were then enabled to deliberate with undivided attention on the surest means of increasing their prosperity and reaping the certain fruits of reciprocal affection." From the very commencement of their sittings, the advantages obtained were considered as victories, not concessions. Sentiments of distrust and alienation suggested the speeches, doubt and suspicion characterised the acts of the Irish political leaders. It was to no purpose that the British Parliament manifested its willingness to satisfy their misgivings, first aroused in the insufficiency of the repeal of Poyning's Law, by at once passing the Act "for preventing or removing all doubts," and in the most explicit terms settling the question. Want of faith in England was the Shibboleth of Irish politicians. The people believed that by Independence they had gained much. Their distresses had hitherto been ascribed to English oppression and misrule. They waited for measures calculated to diminish their burdens and infuse energy into their industries. The Roman Catholics, the numerical strength of the State, anticipated that a free Irish Parliament would give to them that fuller enjoyment of civil and religious liberty, which they believed the sectarianism of England had withheld. Both were disappointed, and both began to murmur. The echoes of their dissatisfaction were heard within the House. Exulting in their success and jealous of their rights, Parliament perpetually dangled the infant Constitution before the eyes of the nation, and neglected the means of securing its vitality and vigour. The spirit of practical legislation was entirely wanting to their proceedings ; prolonged debates leading to no beneficial results. Those outside the House began to think the State infant rather a nuisance than otherwise ; those within found their business interrupted, for its rattle was perpetual. The masses determined, while the child was being quarrelled over by its guardians, to take action for themselves. The Irish people, susceptible and impulsive, had every incentive to action against the English Government, which they believed had been indifferent to their complaints. They compared their present and their past condition, and found no improvement since their Parliament was free. They had many examples which gave them confidence in their resistance to the law. The declaration of American Independence, and the circumstances attending it, had been discussed in every village, where some one of the 4000 Irishmen voted in the Harcourt administration for the American war, had relatives or friends. The progress of Republican institutions in Roman Catholic France, had sent a thrill of hope into each breast professing "the old faith." At home the successful achievements of the Protestant Volunteers was not without its teaching. The Declaration of Dungannon, and the assertion of Independence were so many illustrations of the result of armed opinion. The Catholics of Ireland would have been less than men had they observed these events unmoved. They looked to Parliament for relief and found but little, yet they heard much. The leading men in the senate openly accused England of perfidy and wrong. They regarded all overtures coming from her as covert designs on their constitution. They publicly proclaimed the baseness and corruption of their own assembly, and yet refused to adopt the means within their reach for its remedy. They avowed that the Government had their majority in its pay. Mutual revilings constituted the chief interest of their debates, and yet it was expected that a nation little informed, and unable or unwilling to think and judge for itself, should have faith in an executive which its representatives mistrusted, or give to them that confidence which its members withheld from one another.

In this position the Irish people were too ready to believe whatever they were told by interested informers, and to follow pernicious courses recommended by false advisers for their own selfish ends. Their sympathies were misled by appeals to matters of which they could only comprehend the outline, much less reflect on their importance and tendency. There was no want of genuine and unselfish patriotism amongst many Catholics, who, influenced by love of country, desired to maintain her so-called "Independence," but they required guidance, and guidance they had none, for interests of creed and of country were believed to conflict. There were not wanting agitators, who, at all periods of public disturbance, come to the front, and assume a direction of the masses, who do not reflect on questions they are generally too ignorant to understand. Such, under unscrupulous advice, are ever ready either to intimidate a Government or influence the conduct of individuals. These petty-mongers of their Country's honour found powerful coadjutors, and active and ample elements of mischief, in the great abuses which admittedly prevailed. They addressed men heated with enthusiasm and agitated by love of change. The spirit outside the House, influenced the debates within. The descent from patriotism to faction is easy : zeal for a principle soon begets impatience of opposition, as the desire of victory over an adversary generally leads to power being regarded as an instrument for mere personal gratification. This was illustrated in the Irish Parliament, so that popular following became an essential element of success. The change in public opinion was gradual but sure. The natural tendency of Constitutional doctrines, when embraced with fanatical zeal, is to merge into Republicanism. The brilliant declamations of Grattan, in his exposure of abuses, suggested to many that the opinions and doctrines of the Revolution were the best answer to laws admittedly oppressive, maintained by a legislature known to be corrupt. The conduct of the Government in these critical times was as indecent as it was pernicious, and tended to keep the people in a constant state of ferment and disquiet. Instead of taking a firm and determined course through the majority at its command in Parliament, and adjusting causes of complaint while punishing disturbers of the peace ; they not only neglected due precautions against the arts and acts of violent partisans, but even permitted them to work upon the public mind and to obtain an ascendancy which it was impossible subsequently to destroy. Agitators were allowed to assume a tone of authority and to use language of dictation to a people who had abundant illustrations of what armed opinion was capable of accomplishing ; and this at a time when Europe was being shaken to its foundations, and Ireland was known to be warm in her sympathies and intimate in her associations with France.

The Volunteers had been disbanded. Their Convention in Dublin had conflicted with the authority of Parliament and had been dissolved under the pressure of public opinion, then not altogether alienated from the Constitution. The attempted Congress had been prevented by the strong arm of the law. Government at length had been aroused to the danger of neglecting precautions against the wiles of pseudo-patriots, and it was determined to permit them no longer to gain an ascendancy over the public mind, through despising their power. Ministers had, as against their teaching, taken precautionary measures for the protection of the State, but they neglected the only sure means whereby a despicable or unprincipled agitation can be effectually crushed, or honest dissatisfaction rightly appeased,—they withheld those reforms which the people had a right to expect and the state of the National Institutions demanded. While affairs were in this condition came tidings from revolutionary France :— Alarming disturbances had taken place, more particularly at Nismes, where Catholics and Protestants came into collision, and a great number of lives were sacrificed. The old cry of intolerance was thereupon raised, and the conflict between creeds renewed. Throughout the country distrust revived. The Grand Juries in several counties passed resolutions little in favour of the Catholics, [App. 18.] and yet further concessions were admitted to be justly required, which at the same time were considered unsafe, for property lay on one side and physical force on the other When Mr. Gardiner introduced his Catholic Relief Bill in 1781, Mr. Ponsonby "thought it would be extremely wrong to show any unwillingness to receive the Bill;* a people of such exemplary loyalty had his good wishes." The reasons urged after ten years of independence were based not on admiration but on fear; not on appreciation of loyalty, but on apprehension of sedition.

The opening speech of the Session of 1792, was important from its complete freedom from any special interest. The Parliament and the people each waited for the other to begin; it was understood by both, that the existing state of things could not continue. Mr. Grattan on this occasion inveighed against the

* 1 Par D., p. 201

Government with more than ordinary bitterness, for some new members were present, and the feeling of his recent discomfiture was still strong. He assailed the House, and was not called to order. It is worth while to recur to his speech as having the sanction of Parliamentary utterance, which was unquestioned. [App. 19.]

It was understood that this was to be a working Session and that measures of further relief for the Catholics would meet with the sanction of the Government. The occurrence of the French outrages was most inopportune. These and the atrocities in Paris had cooled the ardour of many. Concession and conciliation had made the food they fed on. Outside the House various schemes of Catholic relief had been discussed, but nothing actually decided. On the eve of the Parliament meeting, the Viceroy had called a meeting of such of the Privy Council as he could most surely trust, and laid before them the instructions of the Cabinet, the principle of which was that the connection between England and Ireland rested absolutely on Protestant ascendancy. The Grand Juries throughout the country had come forward in support of the views of the Ministry. "At the hazard of everything dear to them, they besought Parliament to uphold and maintain the Protestant interest of Ireland, and instructed their representatives to oppose any propositions which might be made for extending to Catholics the right of elective franchise." Thus encouraged, the Irish executive agreed that, in the then state of the public mind, neither the point of arms, nor of the franchise could be carried. It was ultimately decided that Sir Hercules Langrishe should bring in a moderate measure, and Major Hobart speak in its favour. This was far short of what was expected if not promised, and the Government seemed compromised in the matter. A son of Edmund Burke, with little of his father's ability, had been enabled to get himself appointed as a champion of the Roman Catholics. His father's name had procured him access to Pitt, Dundas had also conversed freely with him. Both formed the opinion that his ability was far less than his vanity, and refused him their confidence. He nevetherless reached Ireland with a guarded letter of introduction from Dundas to Major Hobart, which he used as an assurance to many, of his being in the Cabinet secrets. He thereby aroused expectations beyond the intentions of the Government, and he drafted a Bill to give them expression. On the 25th January Sir Hercules Langrishe obtained leave to bring in his Bill, its objects being to open to Catholics the profession of the Law, to permit their intermarriage with Protestants, to restore certain rights and privileges of Education, and to enable them to follow Trades. It came under discussion on the 18th of February. Mr. Burke had a rival Bill which sought for all but complete Emancipation ;* he entrusted it to Mr. O'Hara. Mr. Egan also presented a petition from certain Roman Catholics, "entreating the House to take into consideration whether the removal of some of the civil incapacities affecting them, and the restoration of some share of the Elective Franchise, would not tend to strengthen the State." Mr. Grattan said, "we are governed by the ascendancy of the Treasury," and declared the ascendancy in elections to be simply Ministerial, not that of the Protestant people.† The Bill became Law. Mr. Burke's Bill led to no results, whilst the Catholic petition of Mr. Egan asking for the Franchise was rolled along the floor of the House to the door and kicked out.

The Session was hurried to a close, through the House being burnt; but before prorogation the Solicitor-General brought forward the conduct of J. Napper Tandy, for having "demanded an explanation" for words spoken in the debates, and the House ordered the Serjeant-at-Arms, in vindication of its authority, to bring the offender to its bar.

The association of United Irishmen had assumed very formidable extension. Its numbers were vast ; its avowed object separation. Like the Volunteer movement, it had completely changed from its original constitution. When first formed it consisted chiefly of Northern Presbyterians—they then had nothing secret, nothing ambiguous, nothing inconsistent with the duty of loyal subjects ; now covert rebellion marked its movements. The United Irishmen formed a Catholic Society. They determined that a convention should be held under the sanction

* Com. Jour. 18-92.   † 32 Geo. III. c. 21.

of the Catholic Prelates to discuss therein Catholic rights. It was known to the authorities that armed bodies of men calling themselves a "National Guard," wearing a national uniform, openly paraded in imitation of the old Volunteers. It was believed they were in sympathy with France for the purpose of a revolution. The Dublin Convention, through their aid, hoped to accomplish for the Catholics what the Dungannon Convention had established for the Parliament—Religious Independence! A day was appointed for their meeting. A review of the National Guard was at the same time to be held. The Viceroy had no directions how to act. He appealed to Fitz-Gibbon who, as usual, was equal to the occasion, and he at once issued (9 Dec. 1792) a Proclamation against unauthorized bodies assembling in arms. Riots threatened ; the executive was firm, and adequate force was ready. The review was not held. Disappointed and disaffected, armed bands traversed the streets, crying, "Liberty ! Equality !" and "No King!" but the law prevailed. When its authority was acknowledged, the Convention was permitted to meet. It demanded admission to the Franchise and to Parliament, and prepared a petition for direct presentation to the King.

This condition of public feeling marked the opening of the Session of 1793. The Earl of Westmoreland, in his speech, alluded to disturbances at home, recommended a Militia Bill, approved of the determination the House had manifested to enforce obedience to the laws, and added : "I have it in particular command from His Majesty to recommend it to you, to apply yourselves to the consideration of such measures as may be most likely to strengthen and cement a general union of sentiment amongst all classes and descriptions of His Majesty's subjects in support of the established Constitution. With this view His Majesty trusts that the situation of His Majesty's Catholic subjects will engage your serious attention, and in consideration of this subject he relies on the wisdom and liberality of His Parliament." This occasion is remarkable as being the first prominent appearance in the Irish House of Commons of Major Arthur Wellesley, afterwards Duke of Wellington, who seconded the address, and specially approved of the conduct of the

Lord-Lieutenant in "preventing men calling themselves national guardsmen from appearing in military array."

The Crown had information of the importation and manufacture of arms and ammunition. It was known that, under the semblance of Reform discussion, treason was concocted. To meet the double danger of treason and agitation the Attorney-General introduced a special Act,* "to prevent the importation of arms, gunpowder, and ammunition into the Kingdom, and the removing or keeping them without a license." This at once gave the Executive power against the many so-called Volunteer Corps and "Guards" ripe for revolution. A Convention Bill† immediately followed. It prevented "the election or appointment of unlawful assemblies under pretence of preparing or preventing petitions or addresses to His Majesty or the Parliament." The preamble states "that the election or appointment of assemblies purporting to represent the people, under pretence of preparing petitions, complaints or remonstrances to King or Parliament for alteration of matters established by law, or redress of alleged grievances in Church or State, may be made use of to serve the ends of factions and seditious persons to the violation of the public peace and the great and manifest encouragement of tumult and disorder," and then proceeds to enact that those attending unlawful assemblies shall be guilty of a high misdemeanour. It is a strong proof of the alarming condition of Ireland, that Sir John Parnell's Militia Bill, which provided a force of 16,000 men, and increased the regular troops to 20,000, should, after discussion, be carried without a division.‡

Again was the question of reform introduced by Grattan, now in a less pretentious form. On the 11th of February he read three resolutions :—" 1. That the representation of the people is attended with great and heavy charges and payments in consequence of elections and returns of members to serve in Parliament, and that said abuses ought to be abolished. 2. That of the 300 members elected to serve in Parliament, the Counties and Counties of Cities and Towns,

---

* 33 Geo. III. c. 2.   † 33 Geo. III. c. 29.   ‡ 33 Geo. III. c. 22.

together with the University, return 84 members, and that the remaining 216 are returned by Boroughs and Manors. 3. That the state of the representation in Parliament requires amendment." Against the passing of any Reform Bill the Government was on its guard. Pledged in a measure to the Catholics for their participation in the franchise, Reform was considered as equivalent to placing the country in their hands. The Chancellor of the Exchequer moved by way of amendment : " 1. That if any plan shall be proposed which shall promise additional benefits, without hazarding the advantages we enjoy, it shall be considered to be entitled to the most serious attention of the Committee. 2. That under the present order of representation the privileges of the people have been extended, and the agriculture, the trade, and the commerce of the nation have been promoted." A debate followed, in which leading members of both sides joined, the amendment being carried by 135—71. A similar result attended an attempt subsequently introduced by Mr. Forbes.

The speech of the Lord-Lieutenant had prepared the way for further relief to the Roman Catholics. The Convention had agreed to discontinue their meetings; before doing so a deputation of the United Irishmen had requested an interview and been refused. Major Hobart brought forward his Bill. The House resolved itself into Committee. On the second reading Mr. Knox had moved "that the Roman Catholics should have seats in Parliament." His motion was set aside as inconsistent with the order of proceedings. The Bill was violently opposed by Doctor Diugenan, who stated " that Catholic Emancipation meant a restoration of Catholic forfeited estates, which were still partitioned in marriage settlements amongst the descendants of those dispossessed.* The Bill became law.† By this Act Roman Catholics were admitted to the franchise, to the magistracy, and to the grand juries on the same terms as Protestants. Without the objectionable oaths arms were granted to those with certain property qualification, and with oaths to others of minor qualifications. They were permitted to hold civil or military

---

* Par. Deb.. 27th February, 1793.   † 33 Geo. III. c. 21.

offices of trust ; and without oaths to take degrees in any College except Trinity ; they might be elected as Professor to Sir Patrick Dunn's Hospital, with which is associated the King and Queen's College of Physicians in Ireland. This Act and the preceding, read with those passed in 1782, left little more to be obtained but seats in Parliament and judicial office.

Parliament, notwithstanding being so occupied, found time to pass an Act whereby "Barren heath or waste ground improved into arable land or meadow was freed from tithe for seven years," with a provision that burning surface without the proprietor's consent was not to be regarded as improvement within the Act.*

Mr. Forbes was at length to be rewarded with success. He brought forward his usual motion to exclude placemen from the House. After eight years of failure he found the opposition withdrawn, and his Bill reached Committee. It was considered as a set-off against the loss of reform, and it became Law.† It operated in a manner not to affect present occupants of seats, so that a period of four years remained to Government to mature any plans in contemplation. An Act which may be considered as collateral to this was also passed, by which the Government gave consent to limit the Civil Lists to £80,000 a year, and in which by c. 9 they agreed to limit the secret service money to £5,000 a year.‡ reserving by c. 10 "any sum may be paid to the principal Secretary of State for secret service for the purpose of detecting, preventing or defeating dangerous conspiracies against the State." Both these Acts proved powerful instruments in the hands of the Crown. The Place Bill enabled the office of Escheator for each of the four counties to be available for the vacating of seats in Parliament, as each was a paid office of 30s a year. The other gave discretion without question in the expenditure of money.

It is to the credit of the House that, while thus involved in questions directly affecting itself, it should have adopted Fox's Libel Bill, which had passed in England in the previous Session. This they did in an Act "To remove all doubts respecting the functions of juries in cases of libel," an Act justly

---

* 33 Geo. III. c. 25.   † 33 Geo. III. c. 21.   ‡ 33 Geo. III. c. 34.

regarded as the Magna Charta of the Press. The Session of 1793 was, without further important business, brought to its close.

The active co-operation of Parliament and the energy of the Lord Chancellor had avoided open rupture between the Crown and the people. The Convention and the Militia Bills were for the time equal to the occasion. The sudden change of Ministerial policy in abandoning the Pension and Place Bills soon received its explanation. It was known that a French invasion of Ireland had been determined on. Ostensibly to give strength by the union of parties in face of a common enemy, Portland, Spenser and Fitzwilliam became members of Pitt's administration. Mr. Ponsonby stated in the House: "the Duke of Portland and other members of the Rockingham administration would not have joined Pitt, had the Duke not received ample authority to reform abuses which existed in the Irish Government." To him was confided the general management and superintendence of Ireland ; and leading Irish politicians were invited to England to discuss the position. The Ponsonbies, Grattan, Sir John Parnell and others saw the Premier. The Duke of Portland was not without experience of how little was to be expected from concessions. Grattan's price for Irish peace was the admission of Catholics to Parliament. Pitt was uncertain how to act. He appreciated the necessity of conciliating three millions of people, at a time of grave difficulty, when Irish money and men were both required, and an invitation to rebellion was publicly offered in the event of his refusal. Pitt doubted the efficacy of the remedy proposed, and he adopted a middle course. He induced the King to recall Lord Westmoreland, whilst Lord Fitzwilliam, known to be an ardent supporter of Catholic Emancipation, was appointed his successor. Fitzwilliam informed Grattan that he would proceed to Ireland with full discretionary powers. Grattan returned to Dublin and prepared the Catholics for the complete fulfilment of their wishes. The plan of action was discussed in the English Cabinet. In the eleventh hour a difficulty arose with the King. Fitzwilliam was permitted to go without precise instructions ; he was to discourage Catholic agitation, reserve his opinions, make no promises, and communicate the views of Irish officials for the information of His Majesty. With these general directions he arrived in Ireland, and was welcomed with acclamation. The people were led to believe they had only to persevere in their demands and they would be granted. Mr. Grattan saw again within his reach the opportunity which he had lost in the Buckingham crisis. He, and those who acted with him, persuaded the Viceroy to take decided action. Lord Fitzwilliam believed himself authorized to remove certain servants of the Crown. John Beresford, chief commissioner of Customs, was dismissed, and the Attorney and Solicitor-General were noticed to leave as soon as the proper consent could be received. Fitz-Gibbon, bold and defiant, was for the present beyond their reach. These were acts of the greatest encouragement to the expectant Catholic party. On the 22nd of January, 1795, Lord Fitzwilliam opened the Session. He made a long speech in which he carefully avoided the object for which he was supposed to have been specially sent. The public were content to wait. On the 11th of February Mr. Grattan moved to introduce a Bill to repeal the Police Bill. On the 12th he also moved to bring in a Bill " for repeal of Catholic disabilities ;" leave was given, and Mr. Ponsonby and Mr. Knox were ordered to prepare the same. The hopes of the Catholics ran high. In anticipation of their complete success, the Opposition were ready with any sum asked for. £200,000 was granted for the Fleet ; the defences of the country having now assumed additional importance. In the meantime Beresford had been to England ; he had seen the Duke of Portland, and explained matters to Pitt. He returned to Ireland and resumed his place at the Revenue Board. The Law Officers no longer feared change, but as yet their was no public avowal to indicate dissent. News reached London of the doings on the 12th It was stated that the outlines of Grattan's Bill had been laid before Parliament with the consent of the Viceroy, without previous consultation with the Cabinet. On the 5th of February the King was informed, "to his great astonishment," of the change in Irish Policy. He refused his assent, and justified the objections which had been urged by the old servants of the Crown. He left to Pitt and Portland the alternative of either recalling Fitzwilliam, or of allowing him to remain, forbidden to sanction concessions which it had been declared it was his mission to grant. Fitzwilliam suspected that the Ministers had other views. He wrote to Lord Spenser : " You are thinking of a union between the two Kingdoms as a good to be expected from deferring the concession. Depend on the hope of that, and it will be the union of Ireland, not with England, but with France." On the 21st of February Lord Fitzwilliam was authorised to resign, " the manner being left to his own discretion." It is impossible to over-estimate the effects of this movement. It was asserted the people had been betrayed, that it was expected that the grant of supplies and the redress of grievance swould go hand in hand ; that on the faith of promises, the largest sums ever asked for had been given. Sir Lawrence Parsons said : " It now appeared that the people had been duped, that nothing was to be done. If the British Minister persisted in such infatuation, discontent would be at its height ; the army must be increased, and every man have dragoons in his house." He proposed the old plan of 1779 and 1789,—a short Money Bill : an angry debate with mutual recriminations followed, and the motion was defeated by 146—24. Mr. Conolly proposed Resolutions in reference to the Viceroy, which were carried. [App. 20.]

As might be expected, Earl Fitzwilliam's recall was a sore disappointment to many, and the Catholic Committee at once re-assembled. The dissatisfied of both sides hastened to the city, hoping that in an anticipated conflict they might gain something. Grattan once more saw power slip from his grasp. He condescended to reply to an address in which threats were held out towards any successor of Lord Fitzwilliam. He answered: " Emancipation will still pass ; it might be the death of one Viceroy, but it would be the peace-offering of another."* He declared that, notwithstanding, he would proceed with his Bills, and added, " in recalling Fitzwilliam, England has planted a dagger in Ireland's heart." [App. 21.] Lord Fitzwilliam took his departure from Ireland in the midst of every demonstration of public mourning.

* Plow. vol. ii. February 27. 1795.

On the 31st March Lord Camden arrived as Lord Fitzwilliam's successor. He made his entry without official announcement, so there was no opportunity for riot. As if to give effect to Grattan's observation, a disorderly mob thronged the neighbourhood of the Castle. It had become known that His Excellency was within, and that the Chancellor, Council, and Lords Justices would return to their homes when the ceremony of swearing-in was complete. The outrages intended for the Viceroy were transferred to them. The Primate's carriage was injured; he escaped. Fitz-Gibbon was followed, was struck on the forehead and wounded, and was with difficulty rescued. The mob attacked the Speaker's house and became generally riotous. They were at last fired on by the troops, some few being killed and many wounded before quiet was restored.

The recall of Lord Fitzwilliam led to much discussion. The Catholic party, in the bitterness of their disappointment, were ready for any course which would retaliate on the Government. On the 21st April, Mr. Grattan moved for "a Committee to inquire into the state of the nation;" he reviewed the circumstances attending the recent change of Viceroy, and declared it "to be a shock to the passions and affections of the country, coming at a moment when she was calling forth all her strength to assist Great Britain, under the auspices of a Chief Governor whom she venerated, and just after her Parliament had voted the largest supply which any Minister had ever called for, on the faith of those measures which His Excellency was known to have designed." Mr. Stewart (afterwards Lord Castlereagh), replied in very matter-of-fact language, and informed the House that, on Lord Fitzwilliam's arrival, his confidential friends had declared that no removals would take place. He had listened to the advice of certain men who had given him the most mistaken counsel. They were deceived if they thought that he alone was fit to conduct a mild Government; the present Chief Governor was fully adequate to it; the large supplies had been voted after Lord Fitzwilliam's recall was generally known; and he concluded: "In his opinion, if Parliamentary Reform or the Repeal of the Convention Act were in the contemplation of the late Ministers, he rejoiced they were no longer in possession of power." The motion was lost by 158—18.

Mr. Grattan stood committed to the passing of some measure of Catholic Relief. The Roman Catholic Prelates were in favour of an Educational establishment for their clergy and laymen. The former, they pointed out in their correspondence and petitions, "were educated in France, where they imbibed the doctrines then so perniciously at work. They enlarged on the advantages of their being removed from such influence, and cultivating a sense of loyalty at home."* Their arguments were unanswerable, and their requests not unreasonable. On the 24th of April Mr. Pelham introduced a Bill " for the establishment of a Roman Catholic College and an Endowment for the same." Mr. Grattan presented a petition in opposition, which set forth "the inexpediency of establishing an Educational establishment from which Protestants should be excluded, inasmuch as it tended to perpetuate the line of religious separation." The Catholics having recently been admitted into Trinity College, saw, with deep concern, the principles of separation revived and re-enacted. This conflict of opinion fairly illustrates the difficulty to be encountered in the settlement of such questions. Mr. Pelham's proposals were carried, Mr. Grattan supporting them, and thus originated the Roman Catholic College of Maynooth.†

The Roman Catholic Bill, from which so much was expected, came on for discussion on the 4th of May. During the Fitzwilliam administration it had been designed under the sanction of the Catholic Convention, and had been promised as a measure of complete Emancipation, which would open to Catholics, equally with Protestants, the honours of the State. The recall of Fitzwilliam damped the Catholic anticipations of its being accepted by the House. Mr. Grattan thought retreat would prove more disastrous than defeat, and forced the discussion ; he spoke with the consciousness of a losing cause, and the desperate valour of one who felt it was his last chance of obtaining for the Catholics the redress demanded. He was met by a direct proposition from the Solicitor-General (Toler), " that the Bill be rejected." The issue was thereby narrowed to the question : Were Catholics to

* Plowden, Appendix. † 35 Geo. III, c. 21.

have seats in Parliament? All the old arguments, with the new venom which recent disturbances supplied, were urged against the Bill, but the Commons were neither to be intimidated nor persuaded, and rejected it by 155—84.

Parliament in these critical times had duties beyond the routine business of the House. Secret Committees of both Houses had been sitting to inquire into the causes of dissatisfaction. [App. 22.] Both had reported, and the Attorney-General was well informed of what was progressing throughout the country. He had given notice of his intention to introduce two Bills, one* "To prevent insurrections and riots," and the other† to " Indemnify certain magistrates, and others, who, in their exertions to preserve public tranquillity, had acted against the forms and rules of law." This latter was more particularly intended for the protection of Lord Carhampton, the Irish Commander-in-Chief, who, when the " Defenders " in Kildare attacked magistrates, had arrested their leaders, placed them on board a tender in Sligo, and sent them to serve in the Navy. Mr. Grattan moved that during the debate on the Bill the judges should attend to advise the House ; his motion was rejected. Both Bills became law. [App. 23.]

On the 13th of October Mr. Grattan again renewed his appeal for Emancipation, but was defeated by 149—12 ; evidence that the House was weary of the discussions. On the 14th the Attorney-General asked Parliament to suspend the Habeas Corpus Act, a measure rendered necessary by a threatened descent of the French on the Irish coast, and the known sympathies and correspondence of the disaffected.‡ Mr. Curran described the method of its passing§:—" At two o'clock in the morning the House was moved for leave to bring in a Bill to repeal the Habeas Corpus Act ; at five minutes past two the Bill was ordered to be read a first time ; and after a grave and mature deliberation, the Bill was ordered to be read, and was read a second time, at ten minutes after two. Its preamble was then fully considered and approved of, and at fifteen minutes after two

---

* 36 Geo. III. c. 20. † 36 Geo. III. c. 6.
‡ 17 Par. Deb., p. 80. § 17 Par. Deb., p. 80.

it was laid before Committee of whole House." So impressed was Parliament with the gravity of the situation that, when Mr. Ponsonby moved the Chairman do leave the chair, his motion was lost by 137—7. This Act was relied on as a precedent in late years by the English Parliament for in like manner passing a similar Act.

Again did Mr. Grattan bring forward the rights of Catholics to seats in Parliament, this time as a resolution : " That the admissibility of persons professing the Roman Catholic religion to seats in Parliament, was consistent with the safety of the Crown and the connection of Ireland with Great Britain." The subject, though hackneyed, always led to angry debates. Mr. Knox pointed out, as there appeared no hope of carrying the measure, however desirable, agitating it without success would only tend to inflame. He moved the order of the day. It was lost by 143—19, and was so permitted to remain until the united Parliament finally disposed of it.

In the meantime the disturbances in the country continued to demand the most energetic exercise of authority. It was the occasion when all true patriots should stand by the country. There were those who saw in the difficulties a way to accomplish their purpose. Sir Lawrence Parsons proposed that a force of 50,000 yeomanry should be raised in addition to the forces in the country. Mr. Pelham was too experienced to be so caught, or to entrust arms to, and discipline such an Irish force. He declared " that measures had been taken and concerted with Great Britain by which a large force would, in case of need, be immediately sent over." The motion was lost by 125—23.

A vote of censure was next attempted. It was shown that 16 French ships of the line had eluded the vigilance of the English Admirals. Mr. Ponsonby moved " That His Majesty's Ministers are highly criminal by the neglect and unskilfulness which they manifested in the provision, direction, and application of the naval and military force of Great Britain and Ireland upon the late attempted invasion of this country by the forces of France in December last." Wind and weather were urged in defence of the English Admirals, and by a curious process of reasoning also advanced as an explanation of the French being enabled to to approach so near. It mattered little whether the complaint was well or ill founded, the supporters of the Government had the motion negatived without a division,—in which it was more fortunate than a vote of censure proposed on Lord Westmoreland that had 23 supporters. Again was the Absentee Tax proposed by Mr. Vandeleur, who suggested two shillings in the pound. Mr. Grattan supported it, but it was lost by 122—49.

Rebellion progressed! General Lake had, in March, 1797, issued a Proclamation addressed to the people of Ulster requiring them to deliver up their arms. On the 16th Mr. Grattan gave notice of a motion on the subject. On the 18th Mr. Pelham delivered a message from His Excellency : " The dangerous and daring outrages committed in many parts of the Province of Ulster, evidently perpetrated with a view to supersede the law and prevent the administration of justice by an organised system of murder and robbery, have lately increased to so alarming a degree in some part of that province as to bid defiance to the execution of the civil power, and to endanger the lives and properties of His Majesty's subjects in that part of the Kingdom. These outrages are encouraged and supported by treasonable associations to overturn our happy Constitution." The Message was intended as an adoption of General Lake's proclamation. The debate which followed admitted the urgency for action, but questioned the propriety of the course which had been adopted. The motion was lost by 127—16. The proceedings were varied by an angry personal encounter between Mr. Grattan and Mr. Egan, which obliged the Speaker to interfere.

Mr. Fox brought forward a motion in the British House of Commons and proposed " that an address be presented to His Majesty to entreat His Majesty that he will be graciously pleased to take into His Royal consideration the disturbed state of His Kingdom of Ireland and to adopt such healing and lenient measures, as may appear to His Majesty's wisdom best calculated to restore tranquility, and to conciliate the affections of all descriptions of His Majesty's subjects in that kingdom to His Majesty's person and Government." The motion was opposed.

Curiously enough, the arguments used against it were, that it went to affect the independence of the Irish Parliament; that this independence had been recognised in 1782, and that the interference of the British Parliament could not be now admitted. It was lost by 220—84. Dr. Dingenan brought Mr. Fox's speech under the notice of the Irish House of Commons—1st, "as a false, scandalous and malicious libel upon the Irish Parliament;" 2nd, "as a violent invasion of the independence of the House of Commons;" 3rd, "as a flagitious attempt to excite treason and rebellion in the country," and concluded by moving "that the libel be read at the Bar." The Attorney-General opposed, and moved the order of the day. Mr. Pelham was against the original motion, which made Ministers responsible for the acts of the Legislature. Mr. Grattan ridiculed men claiming to excel the patriots of 1782, as being the same who had defended the strongest and most penal acts of the Government. The order of the day was carried without a division.

Whether Mr. Fox had, or had not, renewed his understanding with the Irish Opposition, it is worthy of remark, that his motion preceded that of Mr. Ponsonby, who, for the last time, brought forward the question of Reform. The motion was opposed by many who argued that in the situation of the country it was not prudent to agitate such a question; that a dangerous conspiracy existed, and open rebellion was practised; that peace must be restored before Reform could be attempted; that the measures demanded of Reform and Emancipation would not satisfy the people; that revolution and separation were the real objects sought for." Mr. Grattan reviewed the situation. His speech was sympathetic and to the point. He criticised the arguments that had been urged against the motion, with the consciousness that his efforts would prove unavailing, through his knowledge of the disciplined majority at the Government command. He concluded what he no doubt meant to be a valedictory address: "We have offered you our measure, you will reject it; we deprecate yours, you will persevere; having no hopes left to persuade or dissuade, and having discharged our duty, we shall trouble you no more, and after this day shall not attend the House of Commons."—(May 15th, 1797).

This famous debate practically concluded the business of the Irish Independent Parliament. The leaders of the Opposition seceded from active participation in the further discussions of the Session. Parliament was prorogued in June, and dissolved by proclamation in the August following.

The new Parliament, notwithstanding the Pension and Place Bills and the Catholic franchise, presented little difference from the old. The absence of a Catholic Relief Bill admitting to the House, had preserved the representation unchanged. The active insurrection in the country so occupied Parliamentary and public attention, that to its suppression all other matters were subservient. Mr. Grattan, who had suffered in health from his continued exertions, did not offer himself for re-election. He published a letter and an address to the citizens of Dublin, stating his reasons for so doing. Dr. Duigenan replied in bitter comments, which led to a correspondence characteristic of the times. [App. 24.] The Government and Parliament were, during the year 1798, occupied by the suppression of the most formidable rebellion, and for that purpose Acts of exceptional severity became a necessity. As public tranquillity was restored, and Parliament could calmly deliberate, it became evident that some radical change was necessary in the administration of Irish affairs. It was then determined to bring forward a measure for the Union of the two countries—a proposal which on many occasions had been publicly discussed. Its announcement occasioned no surprise. In the English House, Mr. Pitt had, after a long debate, passed Union Resolutions. England held out her right hand to Ireland; would Ireland accept it? On the 22nd January, 1799, the subject of the Union was incidentally alluded to in the speech from the Throne. Mr. Ponsonby moved an amendment to the address, "declaring their intention of maintaining the undoubted birthright of the people of Ireland, to have a free and Independent Legislature resident within the Kingdom, such as was asserted by the Parliament of the Kingdom in 1782, and acknowledged and ratified by His Majesty and the Parliament of Great Britain." In thus forcing the question, he found the Government with their "arrangements" incomplete. The debate which followed was the life struggle of the Parliament, the numbers were for the amendment 105 — noes 106 — Majority ONE! When the Report was brought up on the 24th, Sir Lawrence Parsons moved that the paragraph which alluded to the measure of the Union be "expunged." Another long debate followed; on the division, ayes 109—noes 104, giving him a majority of five. It was understood that for the Session the measure would be abandoned. The public satisfaction was great. Addresses were voted to those who had opposed it. It was the work of the Session. The question had been postponed, not abandoned. Every exertion possible to be made was made by the Government to insure a majority in the coming Session. Lavish promises to many, direct bribes to some, ultimate advantages to all. Public law was practically suspended. Martial law prevailed. Meetings were prevented, and petitions set aside, the Acts in force being specially directed against such proceedings. The House assembled on the 15th January, 1800, prepared to support the proposals of the Crown. Mr. Grattan, on the sound of alarm, had again been elected. The speech from the Throne was silent on the great question. It announced the success of the British arms both on land and sea; it lamented the disturbed state of the country, commended the ordinary topics to consideration, and expressed entire reliance on "the firmness and wisdom" of those whose parliamentary life it was about to destroy; —no mention of Union to which special allusion had been made in the speech closing the Session. Sir Lawrence Parsons, in replying on the address, moved that the closing speech be read, and proposed an amendment for the maintenance of Independence. The House was crowded. It was a solemn period in the history of the nation. Lord Castlereagh stated "that it was the intention of the Government to make the Union the subject of a distinct communication; that the question had been given up in the preceding Session to enable the country to decide on its merits;" and he asserted that a great proportion of the country were favourable to the measure. The leaders of both sides spoke to the question. In the middle of the debate Mr. Grattan entered the House, supported, in consequence of illness, by Mr. Ponsonby and Mr. Moore. He took the oaths and his seat amid the indescribable emotion of all present. When opportunity offered, he spoke, but at the request of the House he remained sitting. All the old arguments were repeated and familiar topics renewed. The same spirit was present, but his energies, subdued by illness, lacked their wonted fire. Zeal for his country was chastened by sorrow for the blood that had been shed, and the disorder even then not altogether subdued. His speeches must ever be cherished by the Irish people—but all was in vain ; a majority of 42 were in favour of the Crown. By this majority the Royal Message was steadly supported, and it increased until the Resolutions based on that message ultimately assumed their completion in law.

It would be a most grateful office to give expression to the grand speeches on this historic occasion, and more particularly to those of that great patriot, whose name will live for all time, and whose example is the most precious heirloom of Irish politicians. Now, when more than half a century has elapsed, his memory is still green in the affections of his country. For modern politicians, who believe that they can better estimate the requirements of Ireland than he did, "who stood by the cradle of its Independence and followed it to its tomb," it may be permitted to quote his testamentary disposition, after an experience of twenty years of Union, and a seat in the English House ; when, with prophetic vision, he foresaw that complete Roman Catholic Emancipation for which he had struggled in vain : —" I most strongly recommend that the two countries may never separate, and that Ireland should never seek for any connection except with Great Britain." This was the almost inspired conviction and advice of one whose last written words were—" I die with a love of liberty in my heart, and this declaration in favour of my country in my hand."

We have thus attempted to follow in detail—it may be too minutely—the proceedings of the Independent Irish Parliament. The occasion invites to retrospect, and suggests the inquiry:—What measures of practical good had it passed ? What public benefits had it conferred ? What private grievances redressed ? How had it fulfilled those high purposes for which it was ready to show battle, when the unfettered judgment of Ireland, as expressed through her representatives, entered on its free exercise? If, after the perusal of eloquent and, too often, angry debates, the frigid compendium of the Statute Book be taken as the test, it is to be feared the inquirer will be disappointed; for therein it will be found that, of the many measures introduced, few assumed practical completion in law. The records of the Parliamentary debates, and the motions on the journals of the two Houses, contrast strangely with their ultimate results. Who can deny that both time and occasion offered, when acknowledged abuses were publicly discussed without any practical reform, when grievances were admitted without any attempt at redress, when opportunities for the settlement of great questions were sacrificed to the personal prejudices or the antagonism of rival politicians, rather than determined by the requirements and interests of the State? And yet it was the age of great men, whose memories are hallowed as examples of patriotism and of public virtue! With whom, or where, did the fault rest? The general explanation may be found in the long period of oppression and abject subjection from which Ireland had suffered, rendering the people passive to a degree without example in other countries; and, when the pressure was relaxed and opportunity offered, leading to as violent a reaction. Is this mere surmise? The condition of the Roman Catholics antecedent to the Volunteer formation is matter of history. The sectarian bitterness and prejudices of the King would, to the last, have refused concessions, were it not that his Ministers, having the example of America fresh in memory, with that "provident fear which is the mother of safety," placed before their Sovereign the alternative of revolution or concession, and so procured the Royal assent to the measures of Parliament, when it determined to remove many of those religious disabilities which conquest had imposed, but reason and justice had long condemned. Were these relief Acts, which so immediately preceded to the claims for Independence, the results of generous convictions, or of political necessity? There are those who, without excluding the former, affirm the latter, and declare that, wanting the adherence of the Roman Catholics, the

Volunteer movement would have been counteracted in its demand for freedom; whilst assured, if not of the assistance, at least of the passive acquiescence of two-thirds of the people, Mr. Grattan and those acting with him were masters of the situation. Be this as it may, it is worthy of remark that, though the Declaration of Dungannon concluded with expressions of satisfaction that the Roman Catholic claims had been considered, neither the Declaration of Right, nor the answer to the Address which was the avowal of Independence, had any allusion whatsoever to their claims, perhaps through the knowledge that it would be distasteful to the King. It is also remarkable that, from the acquisition of Independence to the close of the Buckingham Viceroyalty, no further advance was made. Religious toleration seems to have been the offering of political intrigue to numerical power. Such concessions as the statutes disclose are traceable to two periods :—the first, when the Roman Catholics co-operated with the Volunteers in asserting Independence, and were otherwise believed to be loyal, and so won consideration of their claims :— the second, after an interval of ten years, when their numbers were again available for political intimidation, and they were known to be disaffected to the Crown and in league with the enemies of the State. The former concessions were the generous, if not the free, acknowledgments of co-operation by authority that felt itself to be strong, and were rendered as tributes to loyalty ; the latter, as unwilling and guarded concessions the Government were unable to resist, were ceded as palliatives to sedition, since their refusal pointed not so much to revolution as to civil war. The Irish Independent Parliament did everything for the Roman Catholics but open to them the doors of the Constitution and permit them to enter the Senate ; this, by their own act, they were unable to do, for England not only held the keys, but paid the keepers.

What were their measures of social reform ? The Statute Book is all but silent. The Charter Schools received their annual stipends, the local demands as submitted to Committees were fairly attended to ; but the great evils were permitted to go unredressed. Absenteeism was quite within Parliamentary control; measures were possible which, in the then circumstances of Ireland, without unduly coercing the landowners, might have equitably provided for those duties which are correlative to the rights of property.* The Marquis of Landowne, in his speech on the Union, observed: "an honourable and efficient measure might be adopted for taxing the Absentees of Ireland, who had been much complained of; many of them he knew to be conscientious and honourable men, and if equitably taxed they would cheerfully pay the impost." True; an Absentee Tax had been more than once discussed and lost. Distinguished statesmen had been in its favour "as a measure to which the Crown would have offered no opposition." Is it to the credit of the Parliament that it should have been rejected, when oppressive imposts, affecting the hearths and windows of the people, were exacted, while such a source of revenue was available in their substitution? Free from the taxes threatened for non-residence, surely the position of those occupying the land thus forsaken received the consideration of Parliament? Again will the Statute Book disappoint expectation, notwithstanding that the public men of the time, those in office and those in opposition, describe the condition of the Irish agricultural classes, as, "for oppression and poverty, being without a parallel amongst the nations of the earth." There were, it is admitted, meagre remedial remedies; the Lease Acts and the Exemption Act seem to be the sum of Parliamentary proceedings in their behalf.

Turning to their manufacturing interests, from every quarter, more especially in the early period of the Independent Parliament, are to be found petitions, either from distressed manufacturers or decaying branches of trade, asking for Parliamentary assistance. To these a ready ear was ever afforded, and a generous aid extended, but no attempts were made to look beneath the surface, in order to detect and remedy the insecure foundation on which such operative industries rested. And yet there is proof it was not want of disposition to entertain and investigate causes of complaint. On occasions, Parliamentary dignity assumed the function of a township, which was discharged in the spirit of a vestry, as

* 34 Hansard, p. 676.

illustrated in the Sedan-chair investigation! It is not on the successful settlement of such a question that the reputation of the Irish Parliament during this period rests, but rather on the failures in the commercial and Reform measures introduced; the debates on which contrast favourably with the Parliamentary discussions of any nation in any age.

It was no argument in favour of her Legislature that Ireland during these years made great progress commercially and financially. The petitions for aid became less frequent as prosperity increased. The cessation of the war, the extension of trade through the removal of its restrictions, the revival of enterprise, and generally the reaction which ever follows periods of prolonged depression and suspense, operated most favourably in her behalf, supported as they were by the wealth and power of England, then affording an open market to Irish supplies. It was a time for statesmanship to have come to her rescue, and it was expected that it would have done so. Lord Auckland, in his speech on the Union, stated that he had consented to the abolition of the Appellate Jurisdiction* "in the confidence of measures being taken, pursuant to the resolutions and the address, to establish the connexion of the two Kingdoms on a firm and permanent basis. He had relied on a treaty being opened between the two Parliaments for the purpose of arranging not only commercial points, but all the great questions involved in the future events of peace and war, foreign alliances, commercial treaties, proportionable supplies, with the whole immense detail under each of these heads." No such steps were taken, and why? Ireland had those capable of guiding her Parliament and insuring her welfare. The mutual antagonism of her two best friends—Flood and Grattan—deprived her of the efficient guidance of both. They might, by placing her commercial relations on a solid basis, by reforming and encouraging her domestic institutions, and consolidating the sources of wealth, which, from many channels were attracted to her soil, have in her prosperity established the stronghold of her loyalty. They did not

* 34 Hansard. Debate on Union.

do so, and for this reason : Doubt and distrust of England became the party cry of political rivals, and antagonism to each other was their personal characteristic ; and both found their opportunities in the perverted sentiments of a generous, sympathetic, but mistaken people. Co-operation between these two patriots might have preserved to Ireland her Independence, by better fitting her for self-government. Flood, on Grattan's entry into public life, had then great experience. Confidence had been with him a plant of slow growth, while Grattan's impulsive honesty made him credulous and often times betrayed him into excess. Flood was a great statesman—Grattan a true patriot ; the suggestions of the head governed the one, the dictates of the heart guided the other. Their influence in the House corresponded with their individual characters. Flood convinced the judgments —Grattan aroused the passions. There is reason to believe that had they co-operated and, in love of country, merged all their personal differences, their combination would have been irresistible for the stability and good of the Irish nation. The House, under the influence of Grattan, rejected the warnings of Flood. It accepted the shadow of Independence instead of its substance. It was content with the mere admission of rights, and suffered the rights to elude its grasp. It permitted the opportunity to pass of demanding a free Parliament to guide the young life of its new Constitution, which was only possible through a complete change in the then system of representation. He was not wrong who declared that "the jealousy of Patriots is destructive of Liberty."

How true Mr Flood's anticipations proved was evidenced when questions of grave interest arose between the two countries. Mr. Orde's commercial propositions afforded the occasion. It was known that Mr. Fox was strongly opposed to the generous concessions of Pitt. He believed that if the resolutions were rejected the way might be opened to office. The fourth resolution, by a perverted construction, could be used to awaken the jealousy and susceptibility of the country. Both were accordingly aroused to a degree that, in the end, neither Flood nor Grattan could resist. Parliament offered no suggestions to bridge over the difficulty. No Commissioners were proposed to meet and discuss terms of arrangement. The state of affairs predicted by the Duke of Richmond had arisen. A delirium of national vanity influenced the public mind; and the occasion on which "the jealousies and discontents" existing between the two nations, might have been brought to a settlement, was not only suffered to pass, but rejected with disdain.

What can be said respecting the treatment of the question of Reform? The purchase of Boroughs was open and undisguised. Peerages were known to have been sold, and it was arranged on the part of the Irish Executive that the money should be so applied. Bribery, as a recognized institution, had assumed the form of a political fine art. Representation was but a name; management of votes being practically a charge on the Exchequer. Titles, places, and pensions, were the prizes or rewards of political turpitude. These things were not only done in the green tree, but they were proclaimed from the dry: when the Law officer of the Crown, in the very Temple of Justice, threatened the recusant creatures of pay with additional taxation as the further burden of dishonour; well might Fitz-Gibbon's scathing retort—most bitter because most true—be oft-times quoted, resented, but not disproved.

Opportunities arose in which commercial rivalries had no part. The common misfortune of both countries called for action. The mental condition of the King required the appointment of a Regent. The position was not provided for either in the English Act of Settlement, or by the Irish Constitution of 1782. It was an occasion when mutual sympathy might have led to identical action. Again did intemperate haste mark the proceedings of Parliament, and Ireland exercise her Independence in a manner calculated to originate grave complications between the two Countries. It may be affirmed that the House was by conscience justified in its resolution. There is unanswerable evidence to the contrary. What can be said of a Parliament that submitted to the observations of the Attorney-General on the eve of their division on so grave and momentous a question? What of members who, in the last resort of their Country, were alone mindful of place, and who, having signed "the Robin," when their machinations were defeated, could sue for mercy from those whom they proved impotent to betray? Inference from analogy fails to supply an answer, for, of analogous cases, to the honour of Parliaments be it written, there are none! Is it too much to assert that, while many of its members redeemed the character of the Irish Parliament in the exercise of splendid gifts, directed by the highest sense of public virtue, they were yet powerless to terminate a condition which they denounced, and unable to prevent representations from being a matter of purchase, political fidelity a bargain, public faith a question of expediency and the most sacred interests of the State from being regarded as subservient to personal rivalry or the mere acquisition of place?

Irish members were nevertheless sensitive of their personal honour, and quick in their resentments when it was individually assailed. Oftentimes Mr. Speaker had to interfere to prevent hostile meetings for words spoken in debate. They also knew the respect due to them as a Parliament. When reflections were cast on their proceedings, they were prompt to have offenders at the bar, and with dignity above resentment, to reprimand or more severely punish. They vindicated the liberty of the press in their immediate adoption of the Libel Bill, and on many similar occasions gave proof that the good government of their country was within their capacity, even though it seemed to be beyond their attainment. In the necessity of controlling the many for the interests of the few, and the fear that freedom from political restrictions would eventuate in Catholic ascendancy, rests the only explanation of their rejection of Reform admitting Roman Catholics to their House. The fact of the mutual distrust of the two nations, induced the Government to secure a Parliamentary majority, which, when love of country and of place conflicted, too often resulted in a divided allegiance, causing strong influences from without, to be counteracted by weak resolves within, and so yielding to clamour concessions which should have been suggested by justice. Much must also be attributed to the pernicious influence of democratic teaching, and the unfortunate coincidence of Republican successes acting on an excited populace of identical faith.

It is too late to enter into mutual recrimination, and ask, Why did the Government of the day so act? Our duty lies with those who were so acted upon—the majority in the Irish Parliament! What avails it to anticipate what might have been, when we are alone concerned with what was? When left to their uncontrolled judgment the sympathies and resolves of the Irish Parliament were always in the right direction. True to their declaration "to stand or fall with Great Britain," they cheerfully taxed the resources of the country to its uttermost; they promptly passed laws for the suppression of riot and rebellion; they declared their desire to protect and give redress to those who rendered service to the State, and though quick to punish, they were yet merciful to forgive.

Of Parliamentary Government, in its truest, broadest and most practical sense, Ireland, in her latest years of Independence, had none. The greater number of her members were either nominees or creatures of pay. It was in vain that Flood, Grattan, Forbes, Conolly and others pourtrayed their real condition. Majorities were made to order like Court suits, to be used as occasion required. So long as they answered the Ministerial call, it was well; but once independent judgment was exercised, and the fate of Flood in dismissal, or the punishment of others less famous in deprivation of the emoluments of place, awaited those weak enough to be honest, or bold enough to betray.

That such a condition of things could continue was impossible. Union or separation became the alternative! By the one it was hoped numerical differences of creed would be so counteracted as to render safe the completion of religious freedom, while identification of interests would eventuate in a common striving of the two countries for their mutual good; by the other, it was felt that the necessity for re-conquest would prove but a matter of time. The English Government adopted the less hazardous course. It avails nothing now to ask, Did the end justify the means? Ireland had her period of Independence — an Irish Parliament achieved it. An Irish Parliament exchanged it for what was conceived to be the greater advantages of participation in Empire. That period of Independence will, by the impartial historian, be quoted as at once an illustration of her glory and her shame.

APPENDIX

I.
Poyning's Act 10 Hen. VII., c. 23.

"No Parliament be holden hereafter in Ireland but at such season as the King's Lieutenant in Council there first do certify to the King, under the great Seal of the land, the causes and considerations thereof, and all such Acts as to them seemeth should pass in the same Parliament; and such causes, considerations and Acts affirmed by the King and his Council to be good and expedient for that land and his license thereupon, as well in affirmation of the said causes and Acts, as to summon the said Parliament under his Great Seal of England had and obtained; that done, a Parliament to be had and holden after the form and effect afore rehearsed; and if any Parliament be holden in that land hereafter, contrary to the form and provision aforesaid, it shall be deemed void and of none effect in law."

II.
6 *Geo. I., c. 5.* "*An Act for the better securing the Dependency of the Kingdom of Ireland upon the Crown of Great Britain.*"

"Whereas the House of Lords of Ireland have of late, against law, assumed to themselves a power and jurisdiction to examine, correct and amend the judgments and decrees of the Courts of Justice in the Kingdom of Ireland, therefore for the better securing the dependency of Ireland upon the Crown of Great Britain, may it please your most excellent Majesty that it be declared by and with the advice and consent of the Lords spiritual and temporal and Commons in this present Parliament assembled and by the authority of the same, that the said Kingdom of Ireland hath been, is, and of right ought to be subordinate unto, and dependent upon the Imperial Crown of Great Britain, as being inseparably united and annexed thereto, and that the King's Majesty by and with the advice and consent of the Lords spiritual and temporal and Commons of Great Britain in Parliament assembled, had, hath, and of right ought to have, full power and authority to make laws and statutes of sufficient force and validity to bind the Kingdom and people of Ireland.

2. "And be it further declared and enacted by the authority aforesaid, that the House of Lords of Ireland, have not, nor of right ought to have, any jurisdiction to judge of, affirm or reverse any judgment, sentence or decree given or made in any Court within the said Kingdom, and that all proceedings before the said House of Lords upon such judgment, sentence, or decree, are, and are hereby declared to be utterly null and void to all intents and purposes whatever."

III.

At a Meeting of the Representatives of one hundred and forty-three Corps of Volunteers of the Province of Ulster, held at Dungannon, on Friday, the 15th day of February, 1782, Colonel Wm. Irvine in the chair.

"Whereas it has been asserted that Volunteers, as such, cannot with propriety, debate or publish their opinions on political subjects, or on the conduct of Parliament or public men.

1st. Resolved unanimously, that a citizen, by learning the use of arms does not abandon any of his civil rights.

2nd. Resolved unanimously, that a claim of any body of men, other than the King, Lords, and Commons of Ireland, to make laws to bind this Kingdom, is unconstitutional, illegal, and a grievance.

3rd. Resolved (with one dissenting voice only), that the powers exercised by the Privy Council of both Kingdoms, under colour or pretence of the law of Poynings, are unconstitutional and a grievance.

4th. Resolved unanimously, that the ports of this country are, by right, open to all foreign countries not at war with the King; and that any burden thereupon or obstruction thereto, save only by the Parliament of Ireland, is unconstitutional, illegal, and a grievance.

5th. Resolved (with one dissenting voice only), that a Mutiny Bill, not limited in point of duration, from session to session, is unconstitutional and a grievance.

6th. Resolved unanimously, that the independence of Judges is equally essential to the impartial administration of Justice in Ireland as in England: and that the refusal or delay of this right to Ireland makes a distinction, where there should be no distinction, may excite jealousy, where perfect union should prevail; and is in itself unconstitutional and a grievance.

7th. Resolved (with eleven dissenting voices only), that it is our decided and unalterable determination, to seek redress of these grievances; and we pledge ourselves to each other, and to our country, as freeholders, fellow citizens and men of honour, that we will at every ensuing election, support those only who have supported, and will support us therein; and that we will use all constitutional means to make such our pursuit of redress speedy and effectual.

8th and 9th. Expressive of thanks.

13th. Resolved (with two dissenting voices only to this and the following resolution), that we hold the right of private judgment in matters fo religion to be equally sacred in others as in ourselves.

14th. Resolved, therefore, that as men, and as Irishmen, as Christians and as Protestants, we rejoice in the relaxation of the penal laws against our Roman Catholic fellow subjects; and that we conceive the measure to be fraught with the happiest consequences to the Union and prosperity of the inhabitants of Ireland."

IV.

*Resolution of Lords Die Mercurii, 17 Aprilis, 1782.**

"That an humble address be presented to His Majesty to return him our thanks for the most gracious message sent to this House by His Majesty's command, through the medium of His Grace the Lord Lieutenant; and to assure him of our most unshaken loyalty and attachment to His Majesty's person and Government, and of the lively sense we entertain of his paternal care of his people of Ireland, in thus inquiring into the discontents and jealousies that subsist amongst them, in order to such final adjustment as may give mutual satisfaction to his Kingdoms of Great Britain and Ireland."

V.

Copy of a Resolution of the House of Commons in Ireland. Die Martis, 16th Aprilis, 1782.†

Resolved, That an humble address be presented to His Majesty, to return His Majesty the thanks of this House for his most gracious message to this House, signified by His Grace the Lord Lieutenant; to assure His Majesty of our unshaken attachment to His Majesty's person and Government, and of our lively sense of his paternal care, in thus taking the lead to administer content to His Majesty's subjects of Ireland; that, thus encouraged by his Royal interposition, we shall beg leave, with all duty and affection, to lay before His Majesty the causes of our discontents and jealousies; to assure His Majesty that his subjects of Ireland are a free people; that the Crown of Ireland is an Imperial Crown, inseparably annexed to the Crown of Great Britain; on which connexion the interests and happiness of both nations essentially depend; but that the Kingdom of Ireland is a distinct Kingdom, with a Parliament of her own, the sole legislature thereof; that there is no body of men competent to make laws to bind this nation, except the King, Lords, and Commons of Ireland, nor any other Parliament which hath any authority or power of any sort whatsoever in this country, save

* Journal of Lords, 17th April 1782.   † Commons Journal, 16th April.

only the Parliament of Ireland; to assure His Majesty that we humbly conceive, that in this right the very essence of our liberties existed; a right, which we, on the part of all the people of Ireland, do claim as their birthright, and which we cannot yield but with our lives. To assure His Majesty, that we have seen with concern certain claims advanced by the Parliament of Great Britain, in an Act, intituled "An Act for the better securing the Dependency of Ireland," an Act containing matter entirely irreconcileable to the fundamental rights of this nation; that we consider, this Act, and the claims it advances, to be the great and principal cause of the discontents and jealousies in this Kingdom; To assure His Majesty, that His Majesty's Commons of Ireland do most sincerely wish that all Bills which become law in Ireland, should receive the approbation of His Majesty under the Seal of Great Britain; but that we do consider the practice of suppressing our Bills in the Council of Ireland, or altering the same anywhere, to be another just cause of discontent and jealousy. To assure His Majesty, that an Act, intituled "An Act for the better accommodation of His Majesty's Forces," being unlimited in duration, and defective in other instances, but passed in that shape from the particular circumstances of the times is another just cause of discontent and jealousy in this Kingdom. That we have submitted these the principal causes of the present discontent and jealousy in Ireland, and remain in humble expectation of redress; that we have the greatest reliance on His Majesty's wisdom, the most sanguine expectations from his virtuous choice of a Chief Governor, and great confidence in the wise, auspicious, and constitutional councils which we see with satisfaction His Majesty has adopted; that we have, moreover, a high sense and veneration for the British character, and do therefore conceive that the proceedings of this country, founded as they were in right, and tempered by duty, must have excited the approbation and esteem, instead of wounding the pride of the British nation, and we beg leave to assure His Majesty that we are the more confirmed in this hope, inasmuch as the people of this Kingdom have never expressed a desire to share the freedom of England, without declaring a determination to share her fate likewise, standing and falling with the British nation."

VI.

22 Geo. III., c. 53. *An Act to repeal an Act made in the sixth year of the Reign of his late Majesty King George the First, intituled " An Act for the better securing the Dependency of the Kingdom of Ireland upon the Crown of Great Britain."*

" Whereas an Act was passed in the sixth year of the reign of his late Majesty King George the First, intituled 'An Act for the better securing the Dependency of the Kingdom of Ireland upon the Crown of Great

Britain." May it please your most Excellent Majesty that it may be enacted, and be it enacted by the King's most Excellent Majesty by and with the advice and consent of the Lords spiritual and temporal, and Commons, in this present Parliament assembled, and by the authority of the same, that from and after the passing of this Act, the above mentioned Act, and the several matters and things herein contained, shall be, and is. and are hereby repealed."

VII.

From the Duke of Portland, Lord Lieutenant of Ireland, to Lord Shelburne, Secretary of State.

Dublin Castle, 6th May, 1782.

MY LORD,—The confidence I find reposed in me is certainly extremely flattering—I will meet it as it deserves, by continuing to write without any reserve.

Under the impression of the unavoidable necessity of conceding all the points required, for the sake of deriving any real advantage from the possession of this country, I do recommend that positive assurances be given that the alteration of the Mutiny Bill and the modification of Poyning's Law, shall be conceded to them in the form required by their Address; that the 6th of George the First shall be repealed, and that Writs of Error shall no longer be received by our Court of King's Bench; but that, as Great Britain, by these concessions, is desirous not only of satisfying the expectations of the Irish upon all constitutional points, but of preventing every possible source of future jealousy and discontent, she does not doubt of receiving an unequivocal testimony of a corresponding disposition on the part of Ireland, and is persuaded that the Parliament of this country will co-operate in the most effectual method, either with the King's confidential servants, or with commissioners appointed by the Parliament of Great Britain, or through the medium of the Chief Governor of this Kingdom, to settle the precise limits of that independence which is required, the consideration that should be given for the protection expected, and the share it would be proper for them to contribute towards the general support of the empire, in pursuance of the declaration contained in the concluding paragraph of their own Address.—The regulation of their trade is a subject which, I think, would very properly make a part of the treaty, and which, from the dissatisfaction expressed by many commercial persons at the delusive advantages of the Free Trade, would be a very fit and necessary subject for discussion. I need not inform your Lordship that they will find precedents in the first volume of the Journals of their own House of Commons, of committees or agents being sent to England to represent their grievances and obtain redress.

As every letter your Lordship has received from me has progressively reduced the hopes I first held out to you, it will be natural for you to expect that I should assign a reason for supposing that the plan which I have submitted to you will accomplish the event we desire. All I can say is, that, in my apprehension, it ought to accomplish that event. In my apprehension, proposals, such as I have stated, cannot be resisted in Parliament with any effect. They so directly correspond with the wishes of the public, that I conceive that no artifice could induce them to support an opposition to them; the refusal to accede to them, or to appoint commisioners for a Final Adjustment, on the grounds of their own Address, when they should be assured that persons were properly authorized for that purpose, would be such an indication of sinister designs as would warrant your directions to me to throw up the government, and to leave them to that fate which their folly and treachery should deserve. If such should be the sentiments of the King's servants, after using every endeavour to bring them to a true sense of their condition, and of the consequences of such a refusal, I should hesitate as little to order the yacht, and to leave them to be the victims of their own insanity, as I should to say that it would be useless to attempt to coerce them, and that the country upon such terms would not be worth possessing.

Suffer me, my Lord, once more to repeat my most earnest intreaties for a speedy determination. There are passages in the two last letters I had the honour of receiving from you which makes me think that there is little or no difference in our opinions upon this unhappy subject; and let me add, that unless negociation can be entered into with persons properly authorized by the Parliament of this country, and that the object is to go fairly to the bottom of the business, and to form a new system of relation between the two countries, upon the basis of their mutual interests, the character of the present Administration will be lost, and the English Government must be prepared to renounce all pretensions to respect or influence in this country. I am, &c., &c.

(Signed) PORTLAND.

To Mr. ————

Dublin Castle, Sunday Morning.
26th May, 1782.

Sir,—I should be very glad to hear that Lord Charlemont was inclined to accede to any part, or even to the idea of such a plan, as you have been so obliging as to communicate to me. I should consider it as a material step to that situation in which I am sure it is the interests of both kingdoms to be placed; being convinced, that whatever is most like a UNION is the most probable bond of connexion to restore and perpetuate the harmony and prosperity of the two countries.

I am, with great respect and regard, Sir,
Your most obedient humble servant,
(Signed) PORTLAND.

Extract of a Letter from the Marquis of Rockingham to the Duke of Portland, dated Wimbledon, 25th May, 1782.

The essential points on the part of Ireland now acceded to, will, I trust, establish a perfect cordiality between the two countries; and as there can no longer exist any grounds of contest or jealousy on *matters of right*, between the countries, the only object of both will be, how *finally to arrange, settle, and adjust all matters whereby* THE UNION OF POWER, STRENGTH, AND MUTUAL AND RECIPROCAL ADVANTAGE *may be best permanently fixed.*

I observe in Lord Shelburne's letter to your Grace, dated 18th May, he states more reluctance to the idea of Commissioners than I should judge to be a general opinion of His Majesty's Servants; the measure may be a doubtful one; but if it appeared to be the inclination among the leading gentlemen of Ireland, I should think good would ensue.

Extract of a Letter from the Duke of Portland to the Earl of Shelburne, dated Dublin Castle, 5th June, 1782.

I have now stated to your Lordship every matter that I can think likely to come before Parliament, and have further to add, that the desire which is generally and emphatically expressed for a speedy conclusion of this Session, will very forcibly tend to unite Gentlemen in discountenancing any attempt to bring on questions of any sort at this season of the year. I presume your Lordship will be of opinion, that it is not desirable to oppose the wishes of this country respecting as early a Prorogation as the business before them will admit. Nor indeed am I disinclined to recommend it; for the passions of this nation do not appear to me as yet to have sufficiently subsided to let the gratitude which is felt pass quietly and confidentially through that channel which can alone direct it to the reciprocal advantages of both kingdoms.

There is no doubt of Government being able to stop any mischief; but I cannot so readily take upon me to answer for the immediate attainment of the benefits which the liberality of Great Britain entitles her to expect. Unless, therefore, *one very great measure*, which I will make the subject of a separate letter, can be obtained, I submit to your Lordship the propriety of coinciding in the wishes of the Parliament, by putting an end to the present Session, as soon as may be after the return of the Bills from England.

From the Duke of Portland to the Earl of Shelburne.

Dublin Castle, 6th June, 1782.

MY LORD,—The measure which I stated to your Lordship in my letter of last night, as a sufficient inducement for deferring the prorogation of

Parliament, is of so delicate a nature, and requires so much secrecy and management, that I think it unadvisable to trust the communication of it to any hand but my own; and as it is possible that the event may not justify the hopes I entertain, it would perhaps be more prudent to withhold the intelligence which I am now about to give you, until I could transmit the plan *properly authenticated*, for the consideration of your Lordship, and the rest of the King's confidential servants. However, as I feel that I have a right to take credit for my endeavours, and that the Ministers in England equally partake of my responsibility in the administration of the affairs of this country, I am as anxious that they should share any merit that can be derived from our joint conduct, as that they should be liable to any blame to which the adoption of ill-advised or inconsiderate measures may expose them. I shall therefore acquaint your Lordship, that I have reason to hope that I may be shortly enabled to lay before you the sketch or outlines of an Act of Parliament to be adopted by the legislatures of the respective kingdoms; by which the superintending power and supremacy of Great Britain, in all matters of state and general commerce, will be virtually and effectually acknowledged; that a share of the expense in carrying on a defensive or offensive war, either in support of our own dominions, or those of our allies, shall be borne by Ireland in proportion to the actual state of her abilities; and that she will adopt every such regulation as may be adjudged necessary by Great Britain, for the better ordering and securing her trade and commerce with foreign nations, or her own colonies and dependencies, consideration being duly had to the circumstances of this country. I am flattered with the expectation of receiving the most positive assurances from   *   *   *   *   *   * of their support in carrying such a Bill through both Houses of Parliament; and in case such an object could be obtained, I should presume that it would be very advisable to trespass upon the patience of this country to bring it to perfection, even in the present moment. Your Lordship may depend upon the earliest account of my success and progress in this business.

I have the honour to be &c., &c., &c.,

(Signed)   PORTLAND.

From Lord Shelburne to the Duke of Portland.

Shelburne House, Sunday, June 9,
Twelve o'clock at Noon.

MY LORD,—In the very instant of the departure of the messenger with the dispatches accompanying this letter, I have the honour to receive your Grace's of the 5th and 6th.

The contents of the letter are too important to hesitate about detaining him, while I assure your Grace of the satisfaction I know your letter will give the King. I have lived in the most anxious expectation of some such measure offering itself. Nothing prevented my pressing it in this dispatch, except having repeatedly stated the just expectations of this country, I was apprehensive of giving that the air of demand which would be better left to a spirit of voluntary justice, gratitude, and foresight. I gave your Grace confidence for watching the temper of those you had to deal with, and cannot express the pleasure it gives me to find that confidence justified. Bargains and compacts may accomplish little objects—great ends must be obtained by a nobler and more generous policy. No matter who has the merit, let the two kingdoms be *one*, which can only be by Ireland now acknowledging the superintending power and supremacy to be where Nature has placed it in *precise* and *unambiguous* terms. I am sure I need not inculcate to your Grace the importance of *words* in an act which must decide on the happiness of ages, particularly in what regards contribution and trade, subjects most likely to come into frequent question. Your Grace will have every merit I can give you. I have only to assure your Grace of every support necessary to carry this measure, and of the most confidential return to every communication you think the public service may require.

I entirely agree in your Grace's reasons for putting as speedy an end as possible to the present Sessions, unless the measure you have in contemplation can be obtained.

The King is at Windsor, and every one else out of town; I therefore only write the sentiments of

Your Grace's faithful servant,

SHELBURNE.

Extract of a Letter from the Duke of Portland, Lord Lieutenant of Ireland, to the Earl of Shelburne, dated Dublin Castle, 22nd June, 1782.

The disappointment and mortification I suffer by the unexpected change in those dispositions which had authorized me to entertain the hopes I had perhaps too sanguinely expressed in the letter which I had the honour of writing to your Lordship, the 6th instant, must not prevent my acquainting you, that for the present those expectations must be given up. I trust, and am inclined to flatter myself they are only suspended, and that they will be revived when the temper of this country shall have recovered it tone, and acquired that degree of composure which must give it the firmness necessary for effectuating so wise and salutary a measure. Mr. F—— will have informed your Lordship of some unpleasant circumstances which were likely to have happened a very few days before the Adjournment, the traces of which are strongly marked in the Address from the Leinster Volunteers, which I have this day the honour of transmitting to you, but which, I think, are to be attributed to a suspicion of the possible effect of a negotiation.

By the account of the events of those three or four days, and of the timidity and jealousy of the first people in this country, it is clear to my apprehension, that any injudicious or offensive measure may be prevented, but that any attempt to conciliate the minds of this nation to any such measure as I intimated the hope of, would at this moment be delusive and impossible.

VIII.

Copy of Resolutions, 4th December, 1783. 5 Lord's Jour.

1. "That all grants ought to be made in separate Acts, and that the practice of annexing such grants to Bills of Aid or Supply for the support of His Majesty's Government, is unparliamentary and tends to the destruction of the Constitution."

2. "That the House will reject any Bill of Aid or Supply to which any clauses, the matter of which is foreign to, and different from, the matter of such Bill of Aid or Supply, or to which any clause granting money in aid shall be annexed."

IX.

23 Geo. III., c. 28. "*An Act for removing and preventing all doubts which have arisen, or might arise, concerning the exclusive Rights of the Parliament and Courts of Ireland, in matters of Legislation and Judicature; and for preventing any writ of error or Appeal from any of His Majesty's Courts in that Kingdom from being received, heard and adjudged in any of His Majesty's Courts in the Kingdom of Great Britain.*"

The preamble recites the Act of the previous session repealing 6 Geo. I. and whereas doubts have arisen for removing all doubts, &c., be it declared and enacted that the said right claimed by the people of Ireland, to be bound only by laws enacted by His Majesty and the Parliament of that Kingdom in all cases whatever, and to have all actions and suits at law or in equity, which may be instituted in that Kingdom, decided in His Majesty's Courts therein finally, and without appeal from thence, shall be, and it is hereby declared to be established and ascertained for ever, and shall at no time hereafter be questioned or questionable.

The second clause provides for the return of all appeals. Writs of Error shall be returned on application.

X.

Mr. Flood's Bill proposed amongst other Reforms, "That every Protestant freeholder or leaseholder, possessing a freehold or leasehold for a certain term of years, of forty shillings value, resident in any City or Borough, shall be entitled to vote at elections of a Member for the same; that decayed Boroughs should have an extension of their franchise to the neighbouring parishes and include them :—that the suffrages of the Electors should be taken by the Sheriff or his deputies on the same day at the respective places of election :—That the Pensioners of the Crown receiving their pensions during pleasure should be incapacitated from sitting in Parliament :—That every member of Parliament accepting a pension for life, or any place under the Crown, should vacate his seat :—That each member should subscribe an oath, that he had neither directly or indirectly given any pecuniary or other consideration with the view of obtaining the suffrage of an election :— Finally that the duration of Parliament should not exceed the term of three years." The Right Rev. the Earl of Bristol, Bishop of Derry, wished the elective franchise extended to the Catholics. He was a very active politician and a prominent member of the Convention.—(*Memoirs of Flood*. Dublin. Cunning. 1830. p. 247).

XI.

Absentee Tax—Absenteeism had long been admitted and recognized as a substantial Irish grievance. The dependent Parliament under Lord North's administration, had attempted to deal with the question. Lord Harcourt as Viceroy, originally approved, but subsequently changed his opinion as to its expediency. Of its merits no one seems to have doubted. On the first mention of the intended measure in 1773, English Peers, resident in England, but possessed of property in Ireland, at once took alarm. Lords Devonshire, Bessborough, Rockingham, Fitzwilliam, Ossory, were loud in their objections, and were not without arguments in their favour. Their exceptional claims were reasons for clauses, but in no wise affected the principle of the Bill. The tax was then proposed as part of a complete scheme of finance for the requirements of the State. Those interested in the defeat of the measure took up the cry that it was but the prelude to a General Land Tax. It was rejected. In the following year Mr. Oliver proposed a tax of two shillings in the pound "on all rents and profits payable to persons who did not reside in Ireland six months in the year." A warm debate followed. The Equity of the tax was admitted, its policy was questioned. It was contended it would lead to the sale of all estates held by wealthy English proprietors, and similar reasons, with no better foundation were urged for its rejection. These prevailed. The Bill was lost by 120—106, a very narrow escape.

XII.

23 and 24 Geo. III., c. 56. " *An Act for the more effectual Discovery and prosecution of offenders called 'Houghers' and for the support and maintenance of soldiers and others houghed, maimed, and disabled by such offenders.*"

Its preamble states " Whereas divers profligate and evil disposed persons in a barbarous and inhuman manner, houghed, maimed and disabled several soldiers," &c. The Act proceeds to charge the County or Barony wherein offence is committed with £20 a year for those so injured ; it enacts the penalty of death, but one day after sentence, the prisoner between the sentence and execution to be fed on bread and water, excepting the Sacrament.

XIII.

Resolutions proposed at a Meeting of Citizens held in Rotunda, 19th August 1784.

Resolved—" 'That the Constitution of Parliament was unbearable, that the people must have a share in the Representation ; that the Catholics must have the franchise; that a venal and corrupt House of Commons had treated the demands of Ireland with indignity and contempt ; that under the Constitution of 1782, any administration could have a majority, and that there was danger of absolute monarchy.' A Committee was appointed. They reported in the name of an injured and insulted Kingdom, 'that there liberties were insecure, that their chartered rights had been infringed, and the freedom of the press violated ; that the Commons were a hired instrument to pillage an already impoverished and distressed people ; a Congress freely chosen by the Irish nation must meet in Dublin ; the Majesty of the People would then resume its proper influence, and divine Providence, knowing the justice of their cause, would assist them in obtaining their rights.' "

XIV.

Charter Schools.—The Irish Charter Schools were the special objects of Government care. Froude describes them, " as the best conceived educational establishments which existed in the world." They were under the management of trustees and Commissioners ; the former held in grants from the Crown large districts of land. By the 21 and 22 Geo. III., c. 27,

Governors of Schools might lease lands in counties of cities and of towns for a term not above forty-one years, with a covenant on tenant to build and renew from time to time, taking fines, but no school was at liberty to demise above twenty acres under this Act, and the consent of the Primate and Archbishop, Chancellor and chief judges, or three of them, must be had under hand and seal, or lease was void. Many tenants held under these powers for short terms; as their farms increased in value under cultivation, or their terms expired, they were without any redress, should their rents be raised or renewal refused. To remedy this, was the object of the Act.

XV.

Petition from Merchants of Dublin.

"That it is the inalienable and fundamental right of the people of Ireland to be free from the authority of any legislature whatever, save only the Parliament of Ireland; and that any covenant, agreement, or statute containing in any shape or form whatever an agreement that the Parliament of Ireland shall from time to time enact in this country laws which shall be passed in another, is inconsistent with the said fundamental right, and would render the Parliament of this realm the register of another Legislature, would in substance revive and introduce by means of our own Parliament the dominion of another, and would overturn the Constitution of this Realm, and would be a surrender of privileges inconsistent with the limited power of an "Octennial trust."—(*Common's Journal*, vol. 12.)

XVI.

40 *Geo. III.*, c. 100, § 63. "And whereas doubts are entertained whether under any law or laws now existing the Governors of the Workhouse of the City of Cork have at present a power to grant licenses for, or to limit the number, or make regulations for, the government of any coach, postchaise, chair, or sedan. Governors of Workhouses are hereby empowered to license persons who keep hackney coaches, post chaises, chairs or sedans, and to limit the number thereof.

The Act imposes penalties which shall be recovered before Governors of Workhouses, or five of them.

XVII.

Round Robin agreement entered into February 1789, by the Members of both Houses of Parliament in opposition to the Marquis of Buckingham, Lord Lieutenant of Ireland.

We, the Circumscribers, having on the Question of the Regency dissented from the mode recommended to us by the Marquis of Buckingham, and acted agreeably to the rights and sense of Parliament, and the duty and confidence which we owe to His Royal Highness the Prince of Wales and the rest of the Royal Family, do make the following Declaration and Honourable Agreement, that is to say :—That if any of the circumscribing persons shall, in consequence of his conduct upon that Question, or upon the measures necessary to be taken in consequence thereof, be deprived of his office or pension, or shall be made, as has been threatened, the "Victim of his Vote," we agree that we will not accept of such Office or Pension for ourselves, or for any other person, and that we shall consider such deprivation, dismissal, or rendering any Individual the Victim of his Vote upon that occasion, as a reprobation of our Constitutional conduct, an attack upon the public principles and the Independence of Parliament, and that the Administration taking or persevering in such a step is not entitled to our confidence, and shall not receive our support.

27th February, 1789.

J. Conolly.	R. Day.	Henry Grattan.
J. O'Neill.	F. Blyth.	Donoughmore.
J. Stewart.	C. J. Sheridan.	P. B. Daly.
W. Ponsonby.	And. Caldwell.	Henry Hatton.
Geo. Ponsonby.	Drogheda.	Annesley Stuart.
Shannon.	Portarlington.	Ed. Newingham.
Granard.	Moira.	Griffiths.
Ross.	Belvedere.	J. P. Curran.
Leitrim.	Landaff.	Edwd. Crofton.
Louth.	Archbishop Tuam.	H. Burgh.
Cavan.	Sunderland.	H. Langlish.
Grandison.	Farnham.	J. Hardey.
Henry Fitzgerald.	Loftus.	J. Doyle.
John Blaquire.	Clifton.	W. Ogilvie.
An. Browne.	G. Ogle.	Leinster.
James Cuffe.	An. Dawson.	Charlemount.
Burke.	Skeffington Smith.	

XVIII.

At the Spring Assizes for the County of Armagh, 1791, the Grand Jury and High Sheriff entered into Resolutions : " that a rage among the Roman Catholics for illegally arming themselves has of late taken place, and it is truly alarming ; in order then to put a stop to such proceedings and to restore tranquillity, we do pledge ourselves to each other as Magistrates and individuals, and do hereby offer a reward of five guineas for the conviction of each of the first twenty persons illegally armed and assembled as aforesaid."—*Plow*, vol. ii, 335.

XIX.*

" They have not been blessed in England with a succession of Lord Lieutenants' secretaries whose sole occupation has been to debauch the

---
* Grattan's Life, vol. ii. p. 357.

morality of the gentlemen of Ireland. No Minister will venture to tell the gentlemen of England that they must be bought; no man will venture to say that the best Minister is he who buys Parliament the cheapest. Men do sometimes desert and oppose their own party, but not themselves and their own list of measures. A man does not in England publicly cross the House to reverse every part of his conduct, and then hold out his little paw to the Minister like a penny boy. There was, indeed, one man in England supposed to have done so, but he was in England a prodigy; let me add, he had been Irish Secretary in Ireland.

The people of this country supposed that England acceded to their liberties, and they were right; but the present Ministry have sent the curse after the blessing. Hear the curse! You have got rid of the British Parliament, but we will buy the Irish; you have shaken off our final judicature, but we shall sell yours; you have got your Free Trade, but we will make your own Parliament suffer our monopolists in one quarter of the globe to exclude you, and you shall remain content with the right, destitute of the possession. Your corporate rights shall be attacked, and you shall not stir; the freedom of your press and the personal freedom of the subject shall be outraged; and you shall not arraign; your city shall be put under contribution to corrupt its magistracy; and pay a guard to neglect and insult her; the seats of justice shall be purchased by personal servitude, and the qualification of your judges shall be to have borne the suffrage and testimony against the people. Taxes shall be drawn from the poor by various artifices to buy the rich; your Bills like your people shall be sold; you shall see the genius of your country neglected, her patriotism dismissed from the commission, and the old enemies of the Constitution made the rulers of the realm."

The above allusion to " dismissal from the Commission," referred to Lord Charlemount, who resigned the Government of the County of Armagh, a confidential honour which his ancestors had enjoyed since the days of Elizabeth. He considered the joint appointment of another nobleman with him in the Government as an insult.

XX.

Resolutions.*—That his Excellency the Lord Lieutenant, by his public conduct since his arrival in this kingdom, deserves the thanks of this House, and the confidence of the people.

Resolved—That to prorogue Parliament before these grievances, of which the people complained, were redressed, would be highly inexpedient.

Resolved—That the foregoing Resolutions be laid before His Majesty.

* Com. Jour. March, 1795.

There were two other resolutions which were withdrawn.

It was also Resolved—That the Speaker with the House should attend His Excellency with the Resolution. He did so, and His Excellency returned the following answer :—

Gentlemen of the House of Commons,—It gives me infinite satisfaction to find by this unanimous resolution, that my public conduct since my arrival in this kingdom, has appeared to you to be deserving of your thanks, and to entitle me to the confidence of the people.

XXI.

Earl Fitzwilliam did not remain silent. Before his departure he published two letters addressed by him to Lord Carlisle, in which he alleged he was sacrificed to party intrigue. He quoted the secret and confidential communications addressed to him by the Duke of Portland, and did not hesitate to avow what had passed in the Cabinet,—a course which in modern times has been severely censured as being unconstitutional.

" The letters were distributed among Lord Fitzwilliam's friends, and are now in general circulation. One passage is much talked of here. It is a quotation from a confidential despatch of your Grace, in which you say :— that 'deferring this question would be the means of doing a greater service to the British Empire, than it has been capable of receiving since the Revolution. The construction put on these words by many people, though falsely in my opinion, is that the intention of Ministers was to keep the Catholic question alive and in suspense till a Peace, and then employ it as a means of forming a union between the countries."

" (Pelham to Duke of Portland, March 30. Secret S.P.O.)*

XXII.

Report of Lords (Lords Jour. vii. p. 580.) " The attainment of what are called Parliamentary Reform, and Catholic Emancipation were, and continued to be held out merely as a pretext for their (United Irishmen) Associations, and with a view to seduce persons who were not apprised of their traitorous designs, to unite with them." *Report of Commons.* Committee " had discovered that the test of the United Irishmen had undergone a change," a full representation of the people was now their object. The words " in the Commons House of Parliament being purposely omitted," the reason for which has been admitted by three members of the executive examined before your Committee to be the better to reconcile Reformers and Republicans in a common exertion to overthrow the State.—17 Com. Jour. 1795.

* Froude, vol. iii, p. 112.

Form of Oath of United Irishmen (Plow. ii, 536):—

"In the awful presence of God, I ―― do voluntarily declare that I will persevere in endeavouring to form a brotherhood of affection among Irishmen of every religious persuasion, that I will also persevere in endeavouring to obtain an equal, full, and adequate representation of all the people in Ireland. I do further declare that neither hopes, fears, rewards, or punishments shall ever induce me directly or indirectly to inform or give evidence against any member or members of this or similar societies for any act or expression of their, done or made collectively or individually in or out of this society, in pursuance of the spirit of this obligation.

XXIII.

36 Geo. III., c. 20. Resolutions of Attorney-General as foundation of Bill.

1. "That the spirit of conspiracy and outrage which has appeared in certain parts of this Kingdom, and has shewn itself in various attempts to assassinate magistrates, to murder witnesses, to plunder houses, and seize by force the arms of His Majesty's peaceable subjects, requires that more effectual powers should be given to the magistracy."

2. "That (in such parts of this Kingdom as the said spirit has shown itself, or to which there may be cause to apprehend it being extended), it will be necessary that the magistracy should have enlarged powers of searching for arms, ammunition, and weapons of offence and of seizing or securing the same for the preservation of the peace, and the safety of the lives and properties of His Majesty's peaceable and loyal subjects."

3. "That from the many attacks which have been made on the houses of individuals by large bodies of armed insurgents for the purpose of taking arms and money by force, and murdering those who had the spirit to enforce the laws or give information against offenders, it will be necessary that the magistrates have enlarged powers to prevent such bodies hereafter from assembling or meeting either to plan or execute such horrid purpose."

4. "That it will be necessary to give the Magistracy further powers with respect to vagabonds, idle and disorderly persons, and to persons liable to be deemed so, or who have no lawful trade, or any honest means to obtain a livelihood."

XXIV.

Letter from Mr. Grattan to Dr. Duigenan.

Mr. Grattan has seen a very gross, a very unprovoked, and a very ludicrous performance written against him, and signed Patrick Duigenan,

Mr. Grattan don't explain his public conduct to individuals.

The Statute Book and the Journals of the House of Commons are open. Were he to make his public conduct a subject of explanation, it would not be to such a person as Dr. Duigenan.

But as the above-mentioned attack mixes with its folly much personal rudeness, Mr. Grattan judges it not wholly beneath him take some sort of notice of it, and he is sorry to be forced to observe that the author has departed from the manners and language of a Gentleman, and has thought proper to adopt a strain so false, so vile, and so disgusting, as to render Doctor Duigenan a * * * * * * * * too * * * and ludicrous to give an affront or to make an apology.

Mr. Grattan remains in Dublin for three days, and is to be heard of at Kearn's Hotel, Kildare-street.—(Plow. vol. ii. p. 650).

In moving for new writ for Dublin, June 14, 1820, Mr. Beecher said, his principal reason for rising was to mention to the House that a document—the dying exhortation of Mr. Grattan to his Catholic countrymen had been communicated to him (Mr. Beecher), which, with the permission of the House, he would now read.

Finding himself unable to go down to the House, Mr. Grattan dictated it a short time before his death :—

"I have entreated of Providence to give me an opportunity to submit a few propositions, regarding your situation; they go to the Roman Catholic interest and to your own.

"First—I most strongly recommend that the two countries may never separate, and that Ireland should never seek for any connection except with Great Britain.

"My next advice is, that the people of these countries should not look to a Democratical Government; *they are not fit for it;* and the Democracy proposed means *nothing but a Military Government.* Universal Suffrage and Annual Parliaments profess to give power, which *they do not.* Their first operation is to repeal all the laws which prevent the army from voting, and of *course leaves the election to the army.* The next operation is to remove all the laws that prevent persons who are connected with the revenue from voting, and *leaves the election and the influence of the Crown;* the result of both would be a *riot,* and not an election. I have just breath enough to enter my protest against both.

" With respect to the Roman Catholics, they have a right to worship their God as they please, the Roman Catholics have a right to believe in transubstantiation ; they owe allegiance to their God and to their King ; *but they do not owe allegiance to the Pope:* there exists no right, there exists no power to control them under the circumstances. I beg to propose the following resolutions :—

" Resolved—That a Committee be appointed with a view to repeal the Civil and Political disabilities, which affect His Majesty's Roman Catholic subjects on account of their religion.

" Resolved—That such repeal be made with due regard to the *inviolability* of the Protestant Religion and Establishments.

" Resolved—That these Resolutions do stand the sense of the Commons of the Imperial Parliament, on the subject of Civil and Religious Liberty, and as such be laid before His Majesty.

" These Resolutions contain my sentiments ; *this is my testamentary disposition, and I die with a love of liberty in my heart, and this declaration in favour of my country in my hand.*"

www.ingramcontent.com/pod-product-compliance
Lightning Source LLC
Chambersburg PA
CBHW020126170426
43199CB00009B/652